En
is Plenty:

Public and Private Values
for the 21st Century

Enough is Plenty:

Public and Private Values for the 21st Century

Anne B. Ryan

BOOKS

Winchester, UK
Washington, USA

First published by O-Books, 2009
O-Books is an imprint of John Hunt Publishing Ltd., Laurel House, Station Approach,
Alresford, Hants, SO24 9JH, UK
office1@o-books.net
www.o-books.com

For distributor details and how to order please visit the 'Ordering' section on our website.

Text copyright: Anne B. Ryan 2008

ISBN: 978 1 84694 239 6

A CIP catalogue record for this book is available from the British Library.

Design: Stuart Davies

Printed in the UK by CPI Antony Rowe
Printed in the USA by Offset Paperback Mfrs, Inc

We operate a distinctive and ethical publishing philosophy in all
areas of our business, from our global network of authors to
production and worldwide distribution.

CONTENTS

For Robbie, Stephen, David, Cianna and Rebecca

ACKNOWLEDGEMENTS

I write because reading has enriched my life so much. The work of other authors is a valuable gift, which has helped me to take intellectual and personal risks. This book is a response to the ideas and practice of others, and an attempt to keep in motion the gift of their work. Because I write as well as read, I appreciate how hard it is to write well and this makes me appreciate all the more what other writers have given me. Chapters 4, 5 and 6 in particular have a large debt to Aubrey Meyer, Richard Douthwaite, Philippe Van Parijs, Clive Lord, Carole Patemen, Colin Tudge, Anne Goodman, Barbara Brandt and Charlene Spretnak. Some other authors who have inspired me are named in various parts of the text and every one on whose work I have drawn is fully credited in the endnotes to each chapter. From those endnotes, readers can get a full picture of the sources I have used.

My husband Frank Savino has given me the invaluable gift of his support, love and encouragement at all times while I was working on this book. Many others have given me various gifts along the way, ranging from feedback on drafts and proposals, to conversations on various topics from the book, to chance remarks and suggestions for reading. They include: Honor Fagan, Ted Hegarty, Mary Ryan, the late Thomas Kelly, Gina Wisker, Gillie Bolton, Andreas Boldt, Fiona Lyddy, Bríd Connolly, Hilary Tierney, Rose Malone, Joan Ryan, Andrew Herring, Angela Rickard, Fiona Murphy, David McCormack, Eoghan McIlwaine, Tony Ryan, Gerry O'Farrell, Peter McIlwaine, Helen Ryan, Aogán Delaney, John Watchorn, Brian Sheridan, Anne Love, Mary Shackleton, Helen Fallon, Jonathan Williams, Edel O'Kennedy, Eileen Boyle and Rebecca Ryan.

INTRODUCTION

This book is a contribution to a big worldwide movement that involves many people and groups. We are posing serious questions about how we can live well now and in the future, and devising solutions to problems of ecology and social justice. The questions include:

> How can we live in harmony with nature? How do we stop global warming, associated climate change and the destruction of ecosystems?

> How can we eliminate poverty, establish security and sufficiency and provide justice and fairness for all the people of the earth?

> How do we restore an ethic of care for people and for the earth?

> In short, how can we put human and planetary well-being at the centre of all our decision-making?

The book explores how we can all participate in this movement by cultivating a philosophy and practice of *enough* in public and private life. *Enough* applies insights from flourishing ecosystems and from moral thinking to these big philosophical questions about how we should live. Given the crises of ecology, economics and social justice that we currently face, the need for a new worldview is as crucial as new technology. We are all born with the capacity for *enough*; everybody has a part to play in the creation of new ways to understand the world and live in it.

The concept of *enough* is developed throughout this book. I begin here in this introduction, continue in a chapter of reflection, and then move on to chapters showing how *enough* is relevant to public policies and personal resources. The approach I take recognises that the practice of *enough* is not uniform throughout the world; it can take different forms and expressions for individuals and cultures.

Thinking about *enough* highlights how misery, sufficiency and excess differ from each other. Our current economic and social systems discourage thinking about these distinctions. It is usually assumed that we should not put any brakes on accumulation, even if that sometimes means having far in excess of what we need. This kind of indiscriminate growth shows up as an increase in goods or services traded for cash, also known as Gross Domestic Product (GDP). Many economists equate increase in GDP with progress for the human race, even as the great contradictions of global growth politics are becoming more and more clear: the economic systems that provide indiscriminate increase in GDP are harming the resources that sustain us. Economic growth has brought about benefits but its downsides are considerable. The general impulse of growth economics as currently practiced is to exploit resources such as people, land, animals and ecosystems. It is not about serving, fostering, caring for or conserving them.

In the worldview that favors this kind of easily measurable growth, rising levels of consumption, production and cash wealth are all considered to automatically bring about improved human well being. Markets, money, trade, science, technology, competition and profit are good, creative activities in themselves. But with the current emphasis on growth at all costs, they are conducted in ways that are ecologically destructive and morally unacceptable. The world does not have enough resources for everyone to live a consumerist lifestyle. As "standards of living" rise for the materially wealthy, they fail to rise for the less well off. And the means by which we create material wealth and consumer goods often destroy the features of life that make life enjoyable and worthwhile in the first place, such as time for self, family, friends, community, civil society and nature.

Enough has an immediate value in this culture of untrammelled growth. It can help us cope with the personal and social effects of what can sometimes seem like a runaway world. Working out what is *enough* in one's life is a way to get some peace of mind and capacity to deal with hectic daily activities. It is a way to be content, not in the sense of tolerating poor quality, but in the sense of knowing what is valuable and what is not, and relishing the good things we have already. It provides security in times of boom and recession.

But another spin-off of *enough* is that what helps us cope well with the world is also good for us morally and ecologically. If we apply *enough* to our health, finances and personal energy, we automatically restrict the kinds of damage we might be unwittingly doing in the wider world. *Enough* is a concept that is intrinsically moral, intrinsically ecological and intrinsically healthy. Practising *enough* allows us to get what is needed from the world to sustain human flourishing, but without taking too much from individuals, or from social and natural systems. It is also about how to give adequately to the world around us. So it is about the relationship between humans and the world, how we get and how we give. In our modern worldview, we have limited our understanding of how everything is connected to everything else. The emphasis on economic growth at all costs has encouraged us to deny the consequences of always using resources from communities and eco-systems, but never giving to them.

This book shows that the problems are all connected with each other. But just as important, the solutions are also interconnected. A sense of *enough* creates the conditions that will allow a critique of growth. It can also nourish a culture of adapted human behavior, which will give at least some of the earth's ecosystems a chance to renew themselves and at the same time allow social justice to emerge.

In the past, we did not need to make a big deal of *enough*; it was built into our lives in many ways. Our language recognized it in phrases like "enough is as good as a feast", and "waste not, want not". But in modern life the sense of *enough* is badly underdeveloped; in affluent societies we have largely forgotten the wisdom captured in the old sayings. *Enough* is as different as it is possible to get, from our current affluent western obsession with expansion and accumulation. We would benefit from naming *enough* again and exploring its value for us in the future. It is knowledge recognized by earlier generations; its value has become obscured in the world of more, but it can be very useful to us at this time. Knowledge, including knowledge about *enough*, takes many forms; it can take the form of practical skills, interpersonal skills, self-knowledge and critical thinking. All forms are essential, and of equal importance.

Thinking about progress

This book appears at a time in human history when we humans need to make collective plans in ways we have not needed to do in the past. Now we need to plan very seriously, as a global, connected species, because developments have for the most part gone beyond the optimum. We need to make choices that will ensure all aspects of human security, including climate, finance, food, water and peace.

One of the most important choices we have to make is to stop denying or ignoring the consequences of growth. We have never had so much information available to us about the consequences of our actions. We know that we need to reduce demand and slow consumption in the world economy, in order to stop global warming and climate change, and to allow forms of economic activity that would be more life-enhancing than relentless growth. A second choice is even more important: to apply

4

wisdom and passion in acting on the information we have. We need to examine our situation honestly, profoundly and self-reflectively. This is not about inducing a guilt-trip or causing a paralysis of blame, but about acting responsibly.

Part of acting responsibly is to ask what other options are available. We need to ask what is really going on when elected leaders and economists repeat the dogma that there is no alternative to growth. Sometimes they even tell us that we need the money generated by growth in order to sort out the problems it causes. We need to investigate the assumptions implicit in the growth-oriented worldview, and look at who benefits from it and who is disadvantaged by it. Most importantly, we need to ask how we can promote other ways of knowing the world, responding to it and acting in it.

If a tree, for example, continues to grow upwards, it will become unhealthy, unable to support itself, and will topple. A system that grows in only one direction eventually collapses under the weight of its own unbalanced growth. We have seen this happening with the banking system during the financial crisis and recession of 2008 and 2009. Yet the G20 talks about this crisis have focussed on stimulating or "kick starting" economic growth again. Governments are trying to recreate the same type of growth that has already shown itself to be unhealthy.

In many systems, the end to growth in one direction happens spontaneously when optimum growth is reached. In economies and markets, however, this stopping has to be consciously chosen.

It would be easy to dismiss *enough* as a form of stopping progress or even as a naïve attempt to reclaim the past. But if we look with discernment at the modern emphasis on a restricted form of economic growth, we see that it has taken the wonderful concept of growth and given it a very narrow definition: accumulation of material wealth for a few. It has channeled humans' capacity for growth through a very narrow gate. In this channel, the stream gets very fast and turbulent. Survival is difficult and this has resulted in the development of our worst human capacities: indifference, cruelty, denial, a narrow materialism and short-term thinking in an effort to compete with others.

Enough is about creating many different channels for human growth and expansion. A culture of *enough* would judge human progress in diverse ways and not just in the quantitative sense of increasing GDP. Such a culture would always attempt to balance the considerable technical and scientific achievements we humans have made, with an increase in our moral, ecological, spiritual and emotional development. Humane and ecologically sound cultures would be a mark of progress and human advancement.

I have for some time sensed an increase in hope; many people in the midst of out-of-control growth economies have been searching for something better than the modernist obsession with individual material wealth and never-ending accumulation. For many more, who had not previously appreciated *enough*, the recent economic downturns have led them to consider it as a worthwhile philosophy and practice.

This book is based on an optimistic view of human nature. People are capable of appreciating the beauty of *enough*. We can find fulfilment in joining with others to create cultures and laws that make the world secure and humane for all. Humans are motivated by much more than money, although many economists wrongly think that money is the only motivator.

Plan of the book

In this book, I mix very specific proposals for putting *enough* into practice, with more reflective and qualitative aspects. I survey some frameworks for action that have been put forward by independent thinkers and activists, including philosophers, politicians, economists, psychologists, educators and citizen-activists. I also engage in social and philosophical discussion. I have included endnotes to each chapter so that readers can easily trace the sources of the ideas and quotations. For the most part, I avoid names of authors, organisations and activists in the text, since I think that doing so makes for easier reading. But I want to stress my debt to all those whose work is discussed here.

Chapter 1 contains further reflection on *enough* as an idea, examining how it is intrinsically ecological, moral, spiritual and elegant in nature. Chapter 2 examines how, in the drive for economic growth at all costs, we lose sight of limits. We also lose the capacity to distinguish between suicidal and destructive growth on the one hand, and intelligent, ecologically sound and morally acceptable economic activity (including some kinds of growth) on the other. And we fail to recognize economic activity that does not contribute to growth. Chapter 3 continues this examination with a look at industrialization in agriculture, which is probably the single most disastrous choice humankind has made. Industrialized agriculture is incapable of providing food security for the world in the long term. For a while, I resisted writing Chapters 2 and 3 because they go over distressing ground that I did not want to impose on readers. I thought that most readers would know the problems of monetarization and industrialization and would not want to read about them again here. Nevertheless, I later concluded that I should include them, in order to sketch the context that makes a renewal of *enough* so important at this time.

Many readers will not want or need to be reminded of the problems and can skip Chapters 2 and 3 and proceed to the more solution-oriented chapters that follow. Chapters 4, 5 and 6 are about concrete proposals and frameworks for change, based on a philosophy of *enough*. Chapter 4 concentrates on the need to find the fairest process for halting global warming. Given the imperative that exists to reduce the global carbon dioxide emissions that are a huge cause of global warming, the crucial question is how to draw everybody and every country into the process. The answer lies in equity, which has largely been ignored in proposals for change. However a framework called Contraction and Convergence gives equal attention to equity. Contraction is the reduction part of the framework; convergence is the process part. Contraction is about reducing the carbon dioxide emissions. Convergence depends on the notion that all countries should participate in reducing carbon emissions, and that every person in the world has equal entitlements to the atmosphere (part of the global commons) and is thus entitled to "dump" a certain amount of carbon in it. Under a convergence policy, our entitlements would come in the form of a fair quota for each citizen of the globe. Each person could use their quota in total, or trade it in a legitimate worldwide carbon market, without the involvement of a "middle man". Trading by individuals in excess carbon quotas would also provide a type of citizens' income to offset higher energy costs.

Chapter 5 outlines how basic financial security for everybody in the form of a Citizens' Income can contribute to general security and a global retreat from harmful growth, while also encouraging local development. A Citizens' Income also provides a way out of the 'poverty trap', which is a major problem with current welfare systems. The chapter explores who qualifies as a citizen and how a Citizens' Income transcends the left-right political divide.

A Citizens' Income can also benefit employers, because it replaces the minimum wage, which can make businesses difficult to sustain. I also examine how a Citizens' Income can be financed: taxation has been suggested, but there are more exciting possibilities, such as the sharing of dividends from earth resources. The chapter ends with a look at the likely localisation effects of a Citizens' Income, and this theme of localization is taken up again in Chapter 6.

Chapter 6 is about the growth and development of a worldwide food movement, based on intelligent local agricultural practices and the renewal of a food culture in places where it has died out. The basic premise of intelligent agriculture is that food production and food consumption should take place as close together as possible. The chapter cites evidence from around the world that the principle of *enough* can support farming systems capable of producing sufficient high-quality food in each bio-region. Intelligent agriculture is the only approach that is capable of providing food security for all people in the world, indefinitely.

Chapter 7 examines some policy principles that underpin the proposals for contraction and convergence, Citizens' Income and intelligent agriculture. Among those principles are security, deep stability, maximum participation, diversity, resilience and whole-system health. I argue that such principles should inform all public policy.

Chapter 8 examines the role of culture in creating a fertile ground for the introduction of public policies based on *enough*. It goes on to explore the notion of the citizen-leader, who plays an essential role in creating cultural change, which in turn may eventually educate elected leaders and lawmakers. Chapter 9 looks at those human capacities that the citizen-leader can value and cultivate, in order to counteract some of the ways that modern life has stunted human personal growth. It examines critical reflection, the capacity to feel, and an ethic of care. The concluding chapter outlines entry points that readers may choose to the path of *enough*. Mainly, however, this final chapter emphasizes the need to maintain a questioning attitude and to be hopeful about creating a better world.

I have constructed this book in a particular way that was manageable for me. But many other ways were possible. I invite you to dip into the chapters in any order you like. While each chapter can stand alone it is also linked to the others. The book is not comprehensive in the sense that it does not attempt to cover every single facet of *enough*. But it surveys what I consider the best proposals and the most relevant human capacities.

You, the reader and me, the writer

If you are someone who thinks that the solution to our problems is to keep growth going, to make and spend more money, to invest in technology and infrastructure, you will probably have little sympathy with the ideas in this book. If you are one of those "deep ecologists" who envisage a complete breakdown of societies, with famine, war and destruction in the wake of the collapse of the unwieldy growth system, and if you welcome that as "nature re-establishing a balance in the world" with greatly reduced populations, you probably won't have much sympathy with the book either: the ideas will be too ordered and rely too much on global solutions.

The book may speak to you if you are searching at this time. You are probably concerned with finding convivial ways to live well in the world as it is. But you are also open to a critique of the world, in the sense of seeing it with a discerning eye and questioning received wisdom. You are probably also concerned about participating in the creation of better ways of living in the future. You value imagination and diversity and want to embrace the new while valuing good traditions and wisdom. At the same time, you know that the present is all we really have, and you are interested in how we can act now to put ideas into practice in daily life. You are interested in politics, economics, philosophy and psychology in equal measure, because you can see how they are all interlinked.

This book is a tool for reconnecting with your intuitive knowledge of yourself as a moral and ecological being. It is an affirmation of a kind of knowledge that most people have already, but which tends to get lost in the busyness of daily life or the struggle to just get by. It is also a contribution to developing this knowledge in response to our times. If you are motivated and caring enough to ask whether society should serve the economy, or whether economies should serve society, then you are already developing this kind of knowledge.

I write as a middle-aged, middle-class white Irish woman, currently working as a university lecturer. My views are shaped by what I have seen, thought, experienced and done in my life. While that may limit the book somewhat, it does not invalidate the ideas. I am first and foremost an educator and learner and I am convinced of the human capacity to learn and to create something better when a current system does not serve us well. I know that we can develop and grow in many different ways.

My values will come across to you as you read, but I am inviting you to avoid reading this book as my statement of a final "truth" or solution. It is a contribution to the conversation that is already going on about the difficult issues facing the world and its people. The book is my side of the conversation with other writers and activists and with you. I see it as an act of collaboration, through which we can reach better understandings of how we might proceed to create positive futures. The book shows what government can do and what we can do as citizens even when government will not act. Possibility is a hallmark of the approach I take to *enough*.

Throughout this book, there will be break-points where you disagree strongly with me, places where you do not want to go. There may be times when my tone annoys you or you think I am so naïve or "western"-oriented or arrogant, that you cannot read any further. I urge you to not give up on the questions for those reasons alone. If you are surprised or angry at something you read here, if you disagree or if you detect contradictions in the writing, maybe they are the things to reflect on for a while. I am inviting you to explore with me, but also to explore the ideas in conversation with other people. Contradictions and flaws are the places where new knowledge gets made and where we keep good ideas moving and living. Come on a journey with me to discover and create *enough*.

CHAPTER 1

REFLECTING ON *ENOUGH*

This chapter reflects further on *enough* as a philosophy, accessible to all, which can dramatically and permanently alter how we understand and live in the modern world. *Enough* can help us to think in ways that are useful for our time about what is good for human and planetary flourishing, how should we live as individuals and with other people and communities, and what constitutes progress for the human race. And the nature of *enough* is such that it opens up liberating and exciting responses to those questions, without being dogmatic.

Enough does not inspire news headlines. Excessive behavior makes the news and sometimes stories of misery do too. For the most part, however, we deny suffering and misery and put them from our thoughts. We don't dwell on how the world could be re-arranged so that everyone could have sufficiency. We tend to concentrate on excess in others: their spending, their behavior, or their drug habits. And many of us like to carefully tread excessive paths ourselves.

Courage is generally associated with dramatic or traumatic events; we forget that the ordinary also requires courage. We are not in the habit of exploring or valuing sufficiency – it lacks drama, it is too quiet or everyday. A life of *enough* is not usually thought to be successful. Many concede that *enough* is virtuous, but few see it as attractive. It does not draw attention to itself or to people who follow its path. We tend to view *enough* as a way of life devoid of challenge, engagement, adventure or achievement. This leads many to dismiss it as a philosophy for losers, for those who cannot "make it", who cannot read the markets and participate productively and successfully with everybody else. I have conducted public workshops about *enough*, and participants have told me that if they embrace the concept, they fear being seen as penny-pinching, lacking in ambition, anti-money, dull, even mad or irresponsible.

In the modern world, we tend to equate happiness with success, and in turn we define success as material possessions and external achievement. We emphasize constant activity and visible, measurable wealth over experience and reflection. We lack sensitivity to the inherent elegance and beauty of restraint and limits. However, many languages have proverbs or sayings that reflect the insight that enough is as good as a feast. In Irish, for example, the same phrase – *go leor* – means "enough" and "plenty". *Enough* is about optimum, having exactly the right amount and using it gracefully. It is about being economical with what we have, without waste of resources or effort, but without being stingy either. But this knowledge is becoming increasingly obscured.

Generational differences affect how people understand *enough*. For those generations brought up in the early part of the twentieth century, *enough* was a way of life. They tried to instill a sense of *enough* into their own children. Unfortunately, many of those children, now middle-aged, rejected *enough*, seeing it as stingy and associating it with depressed times of rationing and scrimping. And many in their teens and twenties, children of those middle-aged, say that their parents' rejection of *enough* has caused the waste and ecological destruction that is now so apparent.

Whatever our generational experiences, whatever way of life – *enough* or excess – our parents modeled, we all, including children, have the capacity for *enough*. It is part of human nature. We may have to work at developing the capacity, but we all know *enough* when we see or feel it. All of us have had some experience of *enough* – when we had everything we needed at a particular moment. Then, we have known contentment, which is another underrated aspect of human experience in modern times. To appreciate and cultivate contentment is to be open to the value of *enough*.

Many individuals and families are currently bucking the current trend towards accumulation and quantity, and are living rewarding lives based on the principle of *enough*. Some are choosing to do this in community with others, in thousands of eco-villages all over the world.[1] Large numbers of people are unobtrusively living according to a philosophy of *enough*, regardless of whether the world or their national economy is booming or in recession. In towns, suburbs and in rural areas, people are quietly getting the most out of life, cultivating *joie de vivre* without the trappings the advertisers tell us are essential for success and happiness.[2]

Enough does have a presence and a vocabulary amidst the modern emphasis on growth no matter what. Even so, it is a whispered presence: media, education and public debate ignore our collective wisdom concerning human potential for achieving well being by means of restraint and observation of limits. TV soaps don't celebrate *enough* and there are very few novels about it.[3] It is difficult to think of anybody who ever became a celebrity by embracing the concept of *enough*, although Satish Kumar, editor of *Resurgence*, a magazine that promotes the philosophy of *enough*,[4] was a castaway on BBC Radio 4's *Desert Island Discs*. Mahatma Gandhi was famous for a time, for promoting the idea of *enough* as a basis for developing the Indian economy.

Embracing *enough* does not mean that we never experience excess again. There are so many facets to our lives, we probably won't ever be excessive or sufficient in all of them. So it would be a pity to understand excess and sufficiency as having nothing to say to each other. We appreciate *enough* with a special clarity, when we have experienced excess. Excess is sometimes appropriate, although not in the long term. Someone who embraces the harmony of *enough* for the most part of their life will not close off the possibility of excess at certain times and places. Similarly, if we have lacked something such as time or money, we appreciate with great relish having a sufficient amount of it. The trick is for us to know when to stop, so that we do not exceed the optimum point of whatever it is we are doing.

Ideas concerning the beauty of *enough* are not alien or distasteful, although embracing them fully is not a well developed option either because they are so countercultural.[5] Many of us recognize the value of *enough*, yet we receive strong messages to keep growing. In the contradiction between two different messages there lies the potential for wisdom. Striving for *enough* in the midst of a world of *more* is a way to cope with the demands of the modern world. It can help us to balance the different roles we hold and the worlds we inhabit, and to make sound decisions and choices.

Enough and ecology

The words "ecology" and "economics" have the same root; "eco" means "home" or "household". *Enough* takes economics back into the scale of the household, makes it focus on the needs of the systems that sustain us, insists that economics recognize that everything is connected in the wider household of being.[6] *Enough* treats markets, money, trade, science, technology, competition and profit – all the elements of modern growth economies – as good, creative activities in themselves, which can be harnessed for the good of people and the planet if they are kept within moral and ecological boundaries. It distinguishes vibrant economic activity from unregulated economic growth.

Ecology differs from environmentalism, which is a modern way of trying to manage and limit the destructive effects of growth-related activities on the natural world. Ecology is a way of looking at the big picture, including the whole person and the place of humans in the systems of the earth. We need to know more about our home planet, in order to overcome the ways that the modern world separates us off from eco-systems and from diversity. An ecological outlook encourages a sense of belonging, which in turn helps us to create meaning: a meaning that is lacking for many in the cultures that grow up in tandem with growth economies.[7]

Scientific insights into the natural world have made the marvels of healthy ecological systems available to us. They do not waste; they are economical in the original sense of the word; they elegantly and spontaneously observe limits.[8] They are, in other words, truly sustainable. We could take our cues from these organic systems and encourage human, social and economic systems modeled on them.

We should not idealize nature; it can just as easily be co-opted for fascist ends at it can for justice. Everyone wants their ideas to be seen as "natural"; it is a very powerful concept, because it suggests that what is natural is right and unstoppable; it provides a moral justification of sorts. For instance, nature can be employed to suggest that there is a natural hierarchical order of relationships in human society, among different races or ethnic groups, or between the sexes. Proponents of unrestrained global markets and growth economies say that such systems are a natural progression for humans and that there is no alternative to them, even if they sometimes have considerable downsides.

We *can* use insights from the study of nature as a way to examine the kinds of systems that support life. We know that healthy ecosystems are rich in diversity and that they can provide more for their "inhabitants" – human, plant or animal – than impoverished systems, even if both kinds of system have the same nutrient resources to start with. For example, an ecologically run garden has a closed nutrient cycle; nothing leaves it in the form of waste; it uses everything it produces to provide nourishment for the soil and the plants. We also know that healthy systems accommodate growth, but of a cyclical rather than an unlimited kind. Nature favors cycles because they come to an organic end after a suitable period of growth.[9] They do not go on growing because in nature, that is a cancer.

Humans today need to consciously self-regulate. Other species and systems, which have not developed cultures that devalue limits, know spontaneously when enough is enough; humans have to choose it. For economic development to be beneficial, it has to conform to very strict ecological and moral limits. Of course, we will never reach perfect agreement on the question of what the limits should be. But rather than try to set absolute rules for them, the important thing is that we start and maintain a widespread conversation about limits. The full potential of *enough* cannot be seen from where we currently stand in growth-oriented countries; it can only be imagined. Its potential becomes clear only as we travel along its path and put it into practice.

It would also be marvelous if "developing" countries consciously fostered the idea of *enough* as they seek progress for their economies and societies, rather than copying the type of over-development that has happened in affluent countries. It would be a disaster if such over-development were the only definition of progress available. The way of *enough* explores how economic activities can be the servant of humans and of the planet, because inherent in *enough* – along with the principle of sufficiency – are the principles of sharing and fairness – the maximum benefit from what is available from the earth going to the greatest numbers of people.

Enough and aesthetics

To appreciate *enough*, we need an aesthetic sense that recognizes the elegance of sufficiency. *Enough* has a beauty that is completely appropriate for our time. What if the cutting edge came to mean, rather than the ever-expanding of boundaries, the art of walking that edge between less and more, sometimes balancing, sometimes slipping? It would be beautiful and challenging at the same time.[10] Wealth could consist in achieving balance and wholeness, including humor, fun, laughter and creativity.

It is difficult to embrace *enough* and its recognition of limits if we consider them to be about mediocrity or deprivation. The notion of limits has taken on negative meanings within our modern way of seeing the world. *Enough* can put us back in touch with the parts of ourselves that understand the beauty of scale and sufficiency, the parts that empathize with the rest of creation. The arts – the record in music, painting, writing or dancing of what we have found beautiful or meaningful –[11]work with a notion of limits also. The artist has to prevent the work from exceeding itself, from becoming unwieldy or going on for too long. Otherwise the finished product becomes meaningless.

Enough and Morality

Cultural and personal appreciations of the beauty of *enough* are also the start of a moral practice. A conversation about morality – the principles and values that underpin our actions – is essential for a different kind of long-term public culture that does not rest on the idea that we are fundamentally economic beings. The terms "ethics" and "morality" are often used interchangeably; in this book, I distinguish between them, by thinking of "ethics" as the behaviors that result from moral values.[12] Morality, like ecology, examines how all things can flourish in relation to each other. Both are concerned with connection and the effect that different parts of any system have on each other.

A moral quest asks us to consider things we would often rather ignore. It asks us to reflect on the place that each one of us has in this world, the extent of the damage that humans have done in the world and the responsibility that each one of us has for creating a just world: what, in short, are our obligations to other people and to the earth itself? We often don't do enough of this, so *enough* requires that we do more of what we neglect right now. And it requires more than asking what is wrong; it involves going on to ask, how we can behave in ways that are right. Morality and ethics require that we examine the consequences of our beliefs and actions in areas beyond ourselves and our immediate environment, and in the long term.

A lack of moral development is distinct from a breakdown in organized religion. Institutional religions have traditionally held a monopoly on moral pronouncements, and indeed have tended to emphasize the guilt and shame aspects of our private lives. Progressive religious leaders are thankfully recognizing the need to broaden moral understanding, and that is to be welcomed. But we must not leave morality to religions – it is something we all need to concern ourselves with, whether we take a religious view of the world or not. Morality can be thought of as another way of naming politics, since politics too is concerned with human and planetary well being.[13]

World economics needs to be subjected to moral and ecological scrutiny. There is a moral dilemma involved in the way that economics, narrowly understood, has taken away our capacity to live good lives. We produce and consume to "keep the economy going" but in the process, we also destroy many of the less tangible features of life that support and sustain us. "Maximum individual choice" is the big mantra within growth economics: we are promised enormous numbers of choices, which are supposed to make us happy. We often talk about equality as if it means having the right to shop on an equal footing with other people. But many of the choices available are meaningless and cause unwanted and unnecessary complexity in our lives; they are not actually available to all and they often come at a price of ecological destruction and social injustice.

Enough recasts choice as moral decisions that strive for the common good. That means taking into account all other humans, community systems, the earth, and ourselves as individuals or small family groups. This may mean setting limits on certain kinds of expansion and accumulation, because they themselves limit the choices for others. Taking a moral stance forces us to enquire into what is really going on in the world around us, not just in our own private or family sphere. So the moral dimension of *enough* is also concerned with justice and fairness.

Enough and Spirituality

Spirituality involves full and constant attention to and awareness of what is happening, even if this is painful. Full attention is spiritual in a sense that has nothing to do with institutional religion. If we truly pay attention to the present, then we cannot ignore what is going on around us, the social and environmental realities that we are part of. And if we stop denying and ignoring, then we will not be prepared to live with some of the things we see.[14]

A part of spirituality is about gaining peace of mind, and to this end, many contemporary interpretations of spirituality would have us simply acknowledge and accept what we see. But only to acknowledge the world's wrongs is more likely to bring despair, when we realize the extent of the wrongs. The only way to find peace is to resist what is wrong and attempt to do right.[15] The public side of the spiritual path – attention to social and economic systems – cannot be ignored in favor of the personal. Spiritual searching today must be infused with a political flavor if it is to be relevant to the contemporary scene.

Many of us are already searching for peace of mind in the private realm with activities like yoga, tai chi, reiki, meditation, psychotherapy and poetry. Unfortunately, many spiritual activities, as taught or practiced in the west, emphasize the pleasant and the personal and do not refer to a social or cultural search, or offer a sense of the bigger picture. It is not enough to embrace spirituality, if it is only to escape one's own pain. For example, a spiritual celebration of nature, uplifting and healing as it is, is not complete if it ignores the ways that nature is being violated by economic growth, and if the spirituality does not try to defend nature. Spirituality can all too easily become the pursuit of the pleasant, a sort of tranquillizer. It can be used as an excuse for ignoring or denying what is going on in the world.[16] However, ecology teaches us that one part of a system cannot be truly healthy if other parts are in trouble.

Morality and spirituality appropriate to our times bridge the gap between public and private. They are political matters, because both are relevant to the world around us and to our inner lives. An ecological outlook enables us to look at context, that is, the bigger picture or web, in which our private lives are lived. The search for *enough* enables us to broaden our horizons and critique the systems that set the scene for our lives. It brings together resistance to what is wrong in the public domain as well as in the personal; it helps us to see the need for life-giving systems and gives us a desire to work towards them. Spirituality, like morality and ecology, is a recognizing of deeper levels within ourselves and between ourselves and the world.[17] All three are concerned with an awareness that everything in the world relates to everything else.

We cannot know all the aspects of *enough* without actually doing it. It is a way of being in the world, not a simple set of rules for living. It is like a path whose end point we cannot see before we start out. This is part of its spiritual dimension: although we can understand it cognitively in minutes, it can take a lifetime of practice to come to truly know it. But the more we walk on the road or practice the philosophy, the more we become aware of the nuances and value of the practice. So *enough* can be a slow realization along the way, and it can entail dramatic insights or transformations. It can also take the form of new knowledge that nobody has yet envisaged. There are difficult sides to any spiritual way, such as doubt, fear, failure, uncertainty and struggle. These are to be accepted for what we can learn from them; pushing them aside is another form of denial.

Enough has a good history; it is rooted in past generations and has been valued and practiced by several great wisdom traditions, including religions, especially those traditions that have an ecological outlook, and which view humans as part of the great natural systems. Buddhism, Taoism, Jainism, Hinduism, Christianity, and the Ancient Greeks – to name just some traditions — have for thousands of years promoted the virtues of moderation.

Although *enough* does not rely on religious doctrine, it is not rigidly secular either; its spiritual and ecological dimensions take it beyond any view of life and the world that values only material things, or the strictly rational. Spirituality is about who we are when all inessential trappings are stripped away; it also concerns the most important connections we have in the world.

Making progress

Enough is not about trying to retrieve a supposedly better past. While it is in contrast with the dominant materialist-expansionist mentality of our times, it is not about going back. *Enough* is a living concept, in the sense that it looks to how we can make the future positive and actually *construct* progress, while drawing on insights and understanding that have served well in the past. But it is based on the premise that we cannot undo what we have done. The present world in which *enough* could be valuable is quite different from other times when *enough* was valued, such as the medieval era. To-day many forces separate us from our innate sense of belonging to the world, and from our understanding of limits. We have wrought terrible ecological and social destruction but, perhaps paradoxically, the destruction we have caused is the very thing that makes our re-invigoration possible. In some ways, the earth itself, troubled by the damage we have caused, is forcing us to look anew and recognize the need to re-evaluate economic growth.[18]

Humans today differ from previous generations who recognized the value of *enough*. We have developed and evolved; we have marvelous scientific insights and knowledge, which help us understand many aspects of the intuitive knowledge of earlier times; we have also come through a mechanistic era. We are now at a higher turn of the spiral than earlier societies and world-views that valued *enough*.[19] Like pre-modern peoples, we recognize connection; unlike them, we understand that we are part of an open system that is unfolding, not determined, and in which we can participate.[20]

Some of the issues of our times are completely new and very complex. But we have a number of new "tools" at our disposal. We have a truly global civilization for the first time in human history; we can see for ourselves that events in one place on earth affect other parts of the earth. We understand that citizenship is not confined to humans in nation-states, but that we are all citizens of the globe, and, moreover, that we share citizenship with all the living systems of the planet. We have well developed notions of rights and fairness. *Enough* for our times is about who we are and what we are capable of at this time. In responding to the questions raised by *enough*, we can create new stories about what it means to be human, and what true progress and advancement might mean for us. In the process, we acquire new understandings of self, others and the world.

What *enough* is *not*

Hypercapitalism is the latest, turbo-charged stage of capitalist culture and economics and it is the dominant framework for global economic growth today. But *enough*, although it is about critiquing and resisting what is wrong, is not a rant against capitalism, nor is it an argument for a more humane capitalism, or for socialism or communism. To be fair, the philosophies underpinning communism and socialism (generally regarded as a route to communism) have more in common with *enough*, because they are based on the idea of equality and sharing of resources. But the communist and socialist regimes we have known (including China to-day) depend and depended on economic growth and exploitation of the earth, just as much as capitalist ones do.

Capitalism, socialism and communism are economic forms that belong within a modernist worldview. One of the characteristics of modernity is that it tries to quantify everything. So it values only the kinds of wealth that can be counted, such as possessions or money. All three approaches continue to put economic growth centre-stage, because growth has quantifiable indicators like Gross Domestic Product (GDP), that is, increases in traded goods and services. They ignore the more qualitative aspects of wealth, such as human health and well-being, healthy earth systems and thriving community systems. In their best forms socialist or communist manifestos put morality concerning human beings centre-stage, but they are rarely strong on ecology and human dependence on ecosystems.

If we get stuck in arguing about communism or capitalism, or about the differences in approach that exist within capitalism today, we are prevented from finding better ways to live. We need ways of thinking and behaving that are outside a mindset of unregulated growth and therefore outside modernity itself. Within a postmodern worldview of *enough*, all the arguments concerning hypercapitalism, centralized socialist economies, or a more humane and welfare-based capitalism are part of an outdated modernist model. Those arguments rely on the notion that any kind of growth is good. While certain kinds of growth have brought some benefits, past results are no guide to future performance. In its unregulated forms growth has now become a weapon of mass destruction. *Enough* is neither capitalist nor communist, but sane, humane, local with a global awareness, durable, flexible, creative and participative.

Enough, while it is moral, is not about moralizing. To moralize is to over-simplify, to see things in black and white terms, and to preach to others about what they should do. Moralizers (secular and religious) are often fundamentalists who crave certainty and want to establish fixed rules by which everyone must live. *Enough* insists that we stick with questions and principles, which push us into a higher level of thinking about meaning and purpose. Living with the uncertainty provoked by questions can be very hard to do in contemporary modern culture, which likes us to rely on factual information. But reliance on "just the facts" precludes the kind of discernment that we need in order to promote justice and well-being.

Enough can allow us to create new social forms that nourish human and planetary well-being. It is not, however, a form of knowledge that will act like a magic wand to solve all problems. It is not about certainty or prediction; it is not a moral theory in the sense of a closed set of ideas and rules for practice. It is more a principle, which revolves around a question (what if we put human and planetary well being at the centre of all our decision-making?) and a considered response.

Cope, critique, resist and create

There is a sense of urgency about all that needs to be done, but it is impossible to have an overnight revolution and make things instantly different. We have to cope or survive in the present as well as critiquing and resisting what is wrong. And all the time we have to keep an eye to the future and what we could create.[21] We need spiritual and intellectual courage for these activities, as well as persistence and patience, in uncertain circumstances over a prolonged period. To simultaneously engage in coping, critiquing, resisting and creating may seem impossible, because they involve contradictory actions of involvement and transcendence, continuity and change.[22]

But attending always to these four "ingredients" ensures that the means and the ends are complementary; such attention works on the principle that *how* we act is as important as *what* our goals are. There is no real separation between means and ends; means *are* ends. Each theme or ingredient affects our personal and social lives at the same time. They are attitudes or ways of thinking that can simultaneously permeate all we do. The personal and the social cannot be cut off from each other. The path of *enough* is integrative; it promotes progressive personal change and progressive social change as mutually constitutive of each other and focuses equally on both.[23]

For social activists, publicly concerned with morality, ecology and global justice, there is a need to sustain the tension of having a vision, yet living in a world that is so wrong.[24] We need ecological and moral sensitivity; but one of the penalties of such sensitivity is that one must be the doctor who sees the marks of death in a community that believes itself well and does not want to be told otherwise.[25] Even if you are already critical of growth economics and actively engaged in social movements to construct different ways to live, you may find that your personal life is stressful because it is busy and harried. A personal practice of *enough* can help you maintain and renew your energy for the public struggle.

For those who use *enough* solely as a means to cope with stressful lifestyles, there is a need to broaden horizons and understand that we also need different systems in place, which will facilitate vibrant, ecologically and socially sound economic activity. Ideally, we would have top-down initiatives for system-change so that several interdependent factors could change all at once. Individuals cannot bring about these kinds of system changes but we can create a political climate where they will be welcomed and legislated for (see Chapters 4, 5 and 6). People and the culture we create can also bring about significant social change.

Enough is about possibility, which is different from prediction. The future is not knowable and predictable, despite the claims of futurists.[26] But possibility remains open to us because when large numbers of people, working and communicating with each other, develop in their daily lives new ways of formulating problems and responses to those problems, then social change takes place and it can influence decision-making at high levels. The vision of unregulated growth has until recently been very coherent and convincing: greater spending power for everyone, money trickling down from the top where it is generated. I have even heard it said that we need continued growth, in order to create the money to deal with the harmful effects of growth.

The vision of growth has gone sour; it has turned out to be a suicidal practice rather than an intelligent one. A better world is possible only if greater numbers of people ask hard questions such as how much is too much, who decides, who wins and loses in the process?[27] Ecologists, philosophers, educators, business leaders, politicized religious leaders, scientists and ordinary citizens need to come together to promote *enough* and new visions surrounding it. Global warming is one chance to do this and the recent financial crisis is another. Both, of course, are connected to each other and it would be a shame if the crisis of global warming were ignored in the effort to stimulate the kinds of unregulated growth that have caused many of the global warming problems in the first place. Solutions based purely on technology or piecemeal interventions are not the answer; we must repair a sense of morality in the world if we are to truly rise above these crises.

Enough is neither cynical nor utopian, but hopeful. It is based on our potential for good; it is simple but not simplistic,[28] a principled way of understanding and being. We can think about the future in a hopeful way, grounded in the belief that humans can live up to their potential for good and for moral action. The problems facing us are very serious, but if we look only at the extremely hard realities and avoid the language of possibility, then the realities seem just too much, and we slip into cynicism, denial or despair. We need to lay claim to the notion that human beings have the capacity to intervene in, influence and shape the forces that structure our lives.

You may think that I make very big claims for *enough* and related ecological and moral ways of looking at the world. Of course, there is no perfect worldview; anything taken to an extreme will show its shadow side or become dogma. But a reflexive attitude can prevent the way of *enough* from becoming rigid. This means sticking with the questions and not flinching from the challenges inherent in them. *Enough* is a key concept for the 21st century.

CHAPTER 2

WHEN WE IGNORE *ENOUGH*

This chapter proceeds on the basis that if we want to create positive futures, we have to understand the deeper causes of our present crises. Our search for individual happiness, vibrant societies and economies, an end to poverty and inequality, the promotion of global justice and ecological stability, has to include a critique of the forces that have created the state we are in. It is part of the essential four elements: coping, critiquing, resisting and creating.

What follows is an introduction to some features of the global growth-oriented economic system. Many readers will already know much of what is in this chapter, so if you are one of those, the rest of the book will make sense to you without reading the chapter. But for those who want a quick introduction, I have highlighted the issues of monetarization, economies of scale and globalization. This is not to say I have covered all the angles, in the following paragraphs or in the book as a whole. But if I give you a taste for exploring these issues, then I am happy. If you want to know more, I recommend some of the sources that I have drawn on (books, articles and websites are listed in the notes for this chapter), and you will no doubt also find others, once you begin to search.

The contemporary capitalist economic system
Economic growth in the world today is shaped by capitalist culture and beliefs. Capitalism has probably existed across the globe since about the 16th century, and it can take benign forms. The activities of capitalism – money, trade, markets – are not intrinsically bad. But the form of capitalism that now dominates

is not benign, because its chief aim is to accumulate monetary wealth. All moral considerations have been drained from it, and the prevailing value is the unlimited freedom of the market itself. This phase is often referred to as hypercapitalism, to denote its disregard for limits of any kind.

This most recent hyper-capitalist phase began in the 1980s and is the model adopted by most western governments (the USA and Britain are especially aggressive in promoting it), by the World Bank, the International Monetary Fund and the World Trade Organization. In this model, all the countries of the world are being urged to "grow" their economies. This growth model has three major characteristics that contribute to ecocide and poverty: it values money over any other outcome (monetarization), its projects are carried out on as large a scale as possible (industrial-ization), and it takes place on a global stage (globalization). A host of other linked characteristics are also mentioned in the discussion below.

A monetarist outlook

Ignoring limits has reversed an earlier regulatory system surrounding markets and trade, in which greed, avarice, usury and envy were morally reprehensible. A system that recognized *enough* has been replaced by one where the seven deadly sins became the seven cardinal virtues.[1] Everything in this system – human work, objects and values – is assigned a monetary value. Monetary value and financial success become the only criteria for economic decision-making. Anything that cannot have a monetary value put on it is outside the equation. Anything that can be monetarized is drawn into this net. Money in and of itself is a good thing; it is essential for trade and business. We need enough money, and enough of the other forms of non-monetary wealth like personal health, relationships and the natural world. But when we lose sight of *enough* as a philosophy or principle, those multiple meanings of wealth disappear too; money becomes the main indicator of wealth and the chief driver of economic activity.

Some aspects of a monetarist outlook are:

- Human needs will be met in an efficient way by the market.
- Anything that people are prepared to pay for is ethically and morally acceptable (apart from a few standard taboos).
- We simply let the market decide what technologies are promoted, although this precludes real critical consideration of their long-term consequences.[2]
- The market can democratize society. That is, it can make available to the masses – by means of spending money – possessions and experiences that were once available only to elite groups.
- The market can promote and ensure justice through competition and individual choice.[3]
- Spending money is a way to fix environmental and social problems.

Monetarism sees the economy in very narrow terms: the money-making activities of businesses in the global market, nothing else. The economy is actually far more; it includes activities such as caring, voluntary work, growing one's own food, and work in the home. But these become devalued and sometimes invisible because they do not make money. Only when they produce commodities or services that can be bought and sold do they become valuable, because they then acquire a monetary value. "Productivity" is everything in this mindset.

A monetarist mindset gives inaccurate feedback about the effects of economic growth. Increase in GDP (traded goods and services) is equated with increase in human well being. Growth and monetarism complement each other because the more money that is spent in an economy, the more successful that economy is deemed to be. This mindset is capable of recognizing only "hard" facts such as the amount of money circulating within an economy. The system is working as long as money is being made. Thus, if there is a pollution incident, the work of cleaning it up (or trying to) means that money is spent on salaries and equipment. But this contributes to economic growth, which is considered good. The monetarist mindset is not capable of taking into account the eco-systems destroyed by the pollution; they do not lend themselves to monetary valuation, so they are not part of the overall calculations.

Governments assume that the tax take from increased monetary wealth of individuals can be used to improve the social fabric (by spending). This causes two problems: First, they do not tax the really big players or corporations nearly enough, so the middle-income tax payers feel hard done by. Even so, their taxes are not enough to do the work of improving services such as health and education. Second, the destruction wrought by growth cannot be overcome by spending money on the problems; the assumption that it can is an offshoot of the monetarist assumption that money can fix everything.

In creating monetary wealth, other forms of wealth may be destroyed, but this is largely glossed over. When traditional systems break down, they become commodities; that is, it assumed that somebody can set up a service to produce and sell those systems. In the process, a human quality or relationship becomes regarded as a product to be sold on the open market. Consumers can then buy back the things that the growth system has destroyed. Care and sex become commodities that can be bought and sold on an almost industrial scale. This is very different from exchanging care and sex for money on a more human and community scale and it changes the quality of the exchange dramatically. Food becomes another commodity; it was once about relationships (to each other, to the land and to husbandry); now, it is about price.

Monetarization includes the exchange of commodities for

money and portrays personal monetary wealth as a sign of success. If you do not have money and the possessions to show for it, you are a loser in the system. Fighting poverty takes the shape of creating more personal spending power for the poor. In democracies, it is assumed that everyone should become steadily richer in cash terms. Equality is interpreted as universal access to those things that were once available only to the cash-rich. Everything, including happiness, is available in return for cash, goes its logic.

The money market

The emphasis on and importance attached to money have brought about a situation where the most influential market in the world today is not in goods or services, but in money itself, in the form of the stock market. Such activity is based on "investment" funds which are completely severed from real goods or services. For the financial players it is like a game. Their transactions involve nothing more than moving numbers from one electronic account to another through a global web of computers. But the game has real consequences for real people because they can find the company that employs them under different ownership overnight or a national currency destroyed, as in Mexico in 1994[4] and Iceland in 2008-09.

In the past, the mark of a good firm was how it took care of its workers, how ethical it was, and how it contributed to the community it was based in, through times of good profit and none. That mark disappeared as maximum profit to shareholders became the chief criterion of success. Keeping costs down in every way possible increases profits, and it does not matter whether the process of keeping them down involves getting rid of workers, treating animals inhumanely, damaging ecosystems, or putting people off their land. The motto is: keep your stock price as high as possible by minimizing costs and maximizing returns. The market price of its stock is now the ultimate determinant of a company's success. While profit to shareholders remains important for corporations, in recent developments, the *price* of a firm's shares has become the most important thing about it.

Another development is that each day almost a million people – mostly Western Europeans, North Americans and Japanese – go online and engage in extremely lucrative stock-trading activities. For the traders it is like a game, but it means that whole industries are in the ownership of people who are largely indifferent towards or ignorant of the nature of the enterprise they own. Their sole interest is that the return on their investment should be favorable.

For the investors, this trading system means they are like absentee landlords, extremely powerful but without responsibility. This has become the norm, and anybody who has a savings account in any institution will have their money put to work buying and selling shares: either directly or indirectly we are all absentee owners. When enterprises are successful and prosperous, everyone is happy to take a share in the wealth, but when an enterprise runs into difficulties the shareholders, or their representatives, try to sell their shares or complain to the managers that their profits are down.[5]

In the USA in the late 18th and the 19th centuries, government restrained the powers of companies in ways that were morally and ecologically astute. Companies were confined to their own state, they had charters that allowed them to exist for a limited time only; their purpose was to serve the needs of the state, which was set out in what we would now call a mission statement. Company directors were not allowed to hold shares in their own company while companies were forbidden from making donations to political parties.[6]

The move away from a principle of limits has formed an environment where the corporation is no longer restrained. Individual rights have been awarded to corporations in the USA in ways that are not compatible with either justice or ecology. In Appalachia, for example, a coal-mining corporation is currently strip-mining the tops of the mountains with disastrous ecological results. The process is destroying eco-systems, flooding villages and polluting water and soil with dumped waste and run-off. It is literally poisoning land and people. Yet the corporation involved has the "right" to profit, even in the face of the destruction it is causing.[7] And it is backed up by the claim that coal is needed to fuel economic activities, especially in a time of dwindling supplies.

Economies of scale and the global stage

When money is valued over other factors, business tries to create efficiency by reducing financial production costs and at the same time maximizing profits. The best way to achieve this is to carry out all projects on as large a scale as possible. This process is known as creating economies of scale. In turn, it favors the businesses that have the most money to meet the start-up costs of the large-scale, industrial operations.

Economies of scale flourish best when they have a global stage. Markets and trade come to be controlled by the smallest possible number of corporations (as few as the world's monopoly restrictions allow), acting across national borders. Of the world's one hundred largest economies, fifty are now corporations, not including banking and financial institutions.[8] Now, money and goods flow freely across national borders, so the economic practices of globalization connect people who live long distances apart (although movement of the people is not always so free). So our consumption pattern in the North, of goods like beef, chicken, flowers, coffee, chocolate, soy and bananas, directly affects the fate of farmers in the countries where those things are produced.

The World Trade Organization (WTO) was set up, without election, to rule international trade on behalf of the supranational corporations. Its aim is to "reform", in other words to do away with any national or regional laws that limit the activities of money-making activities in a "free market". Reform, also known as deregulation, sounds liberal and desirable, but in effect it creates profits only for a few, while others suffer. National governments get tied in to WTO agreements, because they want corporations to do business in their country and do not want their populations to be left out of the money-making loop. But this is very short-term thinking because corporations can move their operations to other places as soon as the local operation becomes uncompetitive, in other words, when the corporation can do it more cheaply elsewhere. All a government can do is to urge its workers to work harder and for lower wages, to be more "productive", so that they can compete with workers in other countries.

This means that local communities compete against one another to absorb ever more of the production costs of the world's most powerful and profitable corporations. We expect workers – employed or self-employed – and small business owners to be endlessly flexible. The message to them is: adapt or be damned.

It is beneficial that knowledge has been globalized through the internet and other forms of communication. Thus, people can learn about each other and different cultures. But the lifting of restrictions on making money for shareholders has resulted in disaster for millions worldwide. The consequences for agriculture and farmers are especially disastrous, and I deal with this in a separate chapter (Chapter 6). Briefly, though, this system creates poverty and homelessness for millions of small farmers around the world, while its treatment of animals is unethical and cruel. It contributes hugely to the destruction of soil, habitats and bio-diversity. The machinery and fertilizers used, along with the movement of food all over the world, create significant greenhouse gases.

The global economy is possible only because the system has

created subsidies. Until very recently, these subsidies made energy and fuel so cheap that their environmental effects were largely ignored. Overall, the long-distance transportation and distribution (whether for import or export of goods or for waste disposal) that a global economy requires are wasteful and costly. What is more, they are a major cause of global warming. While economies of scale may superficially seem to be efficient, they are inefficient when all the costs — human-justice and ecological — are taken into account.

Some kinds of production, such as aircraft or computers, may indeed work best at a global level. But we need to ask serious questions about the correct limits for globalization. A globalized market results in people all over the world leading more or less the same kinds of lives, and consuming the same kinds of goods and foods. These goods and foods are drawn from a small section of the earth's resources or raw materials. When economies are more local, there is greater diversity in lifestyle, food and other goods and this means that we use smaller amounts of a wide variety of raw materials. Although a global system produces cheaper goods initially, in the longer term it depletes resources. When raw materials become scarce they become expensive, making the final products expensive in the long run. But by then, many local economies have been destroyed because they have been flooded with cheap goods from a global market.

Travel for cultural and educational reasons is undoubtedly good. But the globalization of economic activities has created monocultures. It has not led to a consciousness of the importance of diversity, nor of connections in the world at large and how our actions affect other living beings.

Who is in charge?

This economy emerged out of the drive for monetary profit and associated industrialization and globalization. It is probably the case that nobody planned it from the outset. Nevertheless, some people are definitely more powerful than others within the system although they might not admit to being in charge. These include the politicians in government in powerful countries, financiers, banks, the World Bank and the International Monetary fund, industrial companies, and most especially transnational corporations. Closely allied with all of these are economists, scientists and technologists. The body that has the most organizational power to put this corporatized global industrialization into practice is the WTO.

The institutions of monetarist capitalism are fundamentally undemocratic and extremely powerful; if any government wanted to challenge them (and not many do in the west), they would find it well nigh impossible. For example, in Britain the Bank of England forced successive Labour governments to adopt policies to which they were fundamentally opposed.[9] (New Labour voluntarily adopted such policies.)

Most of the individuals who are influential deny their own power and responsibility.[10] Those who have most power within the system are very good at playing it down, at making it seem as if the system has evolved to meet the needs of western consumers. Politicians say that they represent the public will, on the basis that they were democratically elected by the consumers. Company bosses say that they are simply responding to consumer demand. The western voter-consumer, then, is reputed to be the driver of this system and is often called the "sovereign consumer". Growth happens, apparently, because it is the collective will of consumers whose wants can never be satisfied. In other words, they are portrayed as having no capacity for *enough*. This is drivel; companies spend millions developing and advertising products. Why would they need to create new products and then advertise to us, if we are driving the demand?[11]

Consumers are actually pawns in the game. We are required

on the one hand to produce goods and services in our roles as workers; on the other hand, we must consume, in order to provide a market for the goods and services provided by other workers. We are also encouraged to borrow money to increase our buying power. This cycle of producing-earning-borrowing-spending is called "keeping the economy going" and it is part of being a good citizen, in the growth mindset. In recession, when it becomes harder to get credit, governments often are urged to lower taxes, so that citizens will still have money to spend on things they do not need. This is called "stimulating consumer confidence", in order to maintain an increase in GDP. Since the recession and related credit squeeze of 2008, much of the mainstream talk about global rescue packages is focused on re-starting the financial institutions that support this borrowing and spending activity.

The individual who does not produce or consume is of no use to this system. The processes of global, monetarized and corporate growth exclude millions of people all over the world, whose daily activities do not contribute to GDP. A stark illus-tration of this could be seen in Thailand and India in the wake of the December 2004 tsunami: less than three weeks after the catastrophe in their region, those national economies were continuing to show increases in GDP. The majority of the people affected by the catastrophe were the poor, who do not figure in the official economic life of their countries, because they do not contribute to GDP. They have neither jobs to produce goods, nor cash with which to buy them. Therefore, they are not valued in the schemes of government or of big business; they are part of an invisible economy.

But if they can stay on their land and produce and consume the food they need, have access to clean water and other basics, they are not actually poor. They may live on less than two dollars a day, and a monetarist mentality sees them as poor because they have so little cash. But contrast them with those in the pockets of poverty in the so-called first world countries.[12] The problems of the "peasants" arise when government economic policies that encourage growth exclude them from the land that supports them, or destroy the resources that allow people to live well with little cash.[13] Poverty is not an initial state of human progress from which to escape. It is a final state people fall into when one-sided development destroys the ecological and social systems that have maintained the life, health and sustenance of people and the planet for ages.[14]

Global inequality is not all about cash, although a small amount of cash is always necessary to provide things one cannot provide for oneself. Inequality is about the destruction of other forms of wealth (soil, land, climate, communities, systems that developed over thousands of years), in the pursuit of monetary wealth. At first, these destructions hit those without cash the hardest; people with cash can continue to buy from elsewhere things that have been destroyed in their own locality. But eventually those things run out in other places as well. The cash-rich will for a while at least give charity to the displaced or those suffering from other losses, in the form of aid. But mostly we will ask the dispossessed to believe that money is the solution to their difficulties and that they should join the global growth system and earn money, even though the system does not have room for all of them.

We cannot try to alleviate poverty without looking at how it is intimately caught up with the creation of wealth and privilege. When monetary wealth is so important, poverty also comes to be seen in monetary terms. And since not everyone can participate in the money-making economy, poverty cannot be eliminated, it can only be contained. The more we encourage monetarization and take GDP to be a measure of wealth, the more we condemn the majority to be poor in every way, not just financially.[15] Sustained economic growth, conducted on a global stage without stringent regulation and a parallel balance of local economic activity, creates monetary wealth for some. But it is not compatible with the goal of creating economically just and environmentally stable societies.

Who benefits?

The benefits are hollow for everyone in the long term, because of the ecological destruction and insecurity that arise. Some people are undoubtedly making money in the short term. They are the *stratos*, because they live in a different stratosphere from the workers who are pawns of the system, and those who are outside it altogether.[16] Such beneficiaries claim that growth is "flattening" the world, in other words, that it is making the world a more equal place and that an explosion of technologies connects knowledge and resources all over the world, making people equal. But such conclusions are based on the experiences of a very small number of people and, ultimately, millions are left out of this process.

Vandana Shiva argues that the flatness belongs to the vision behind the global growth economy. "Far from flattening and equalizing, corporate globalization is a project for polarizing and dividing people ... never before in human history has the gap between those who labor and those who accumulate wealth without labor been greater. The 'flatness', which writers like Thomas Friedmann see as equality, is accurate only as a description of the social and ecological destruction caused by deregulated commerce – so-called free trade".[17]

The corporate global growth system needs inequality, because there is not enough for everyone in the world to consume at the rate of the "advanced" countries. It needs those hordes of economically "useless" people to stay outside it. Most of them are in the South; we can send them aid from time to time, but ultimately, the more that die of AIDS, malaria and hunger, and the fewer that are born, the better for the system. Susan George has brilliantly exposed this logic for preserving the system in *The*

Lugano Report.[18]

Hollow benefits in affluent countries too

Many would say that it is wrong to argue that only an elite few benefit from growth. But even affluent countries find that growth does not bring everybody into the moneymaking net. Thus, states relying on growth will always have to do something in order to manage poverty-related crime and welfare fraud. In affluent countries worldwide, there are increasing calls for prison places and it is mostly the poor and disadvantaged who end up in prison. The "services" for containment such as security companies, police and military forces add to GDP. They also cost money, so governments need further growth to pay for them.

The need to manage and contain certain segments of the population amounts to a tacit admission that the system that ignores limits and *enough* is not as good as its proponents claim, and that it cannot serve everybody well; it is incapable of creating equality, justice and happiness for all. But rather than mount a critique of the overall system, we are encouraged to believe that the fault lies with corrupt or lazy individuals, and that it is only "natural" that there should be suffering, inequality and corruption. Nature, we are told, is brutal and cruel, and we can expect our systems to be like that too.

There is an optimum range for decision-making chains. But the decision-making chains that result from globalized and industrialized economics are so long-distance that they result in a transfer of power to such a lofty level that citizens' voices sound faint and far away.[19] This makes many people feel powerless and cynical and encourages them to retreat further into private life. Politics aimed at social engagement and the creation of better systems become deeply unpopular. In affluent countries we frequently become shut off from other people in our cars and home entertainment and, especially in the suburbs, the idea of public space disappears; there are few town centers where citizens can congregate to demonstrate, protest or communicate (think, for instance of the large shopping malls that many planners now call "town centers"; anyone who gathers simply to talk, or who gets up on a soap-box in such places will soon be ejected by security guards).

Work

Work is one of the chief ways in which we engage with the world. But many people have lost a sense of limits concerning work, as we have forgotten about *enough*. The logic goes that, in order to keep the economy growing, everybody should do paid work. In many cases, paid work becomes the most important thing in peoples' lives, to such an extent that the workplace comes to "own the soul" of its workers. In corporate organizations, the "most professional" staff members are often those who have learned to subordinate personal goals and moral considerations in favor of their company or institution. In our efforts to create meaningful lives – as producers and consumers, professionals and bureaucrats, workers and members of families – we too often become agents of ecological devastation.[20] Our very sense of ourselves is tied into organizations and institutions that contribute to injustice and ecocide. While we don't set out to do social or environmental damage, we become accomplices in practices that have just those effects.

Once, work and play were distinctly separate. Most people did not overtly bring their passion, multiple intelligences, emotional intelligence, imagination, creativity, or spirituality to their jobs. Quite rightly, many people began to critique that situation, because all parts of our lives are connected. Many workers brought more of themselves to their jobs only to find their personal qualities used to increase company productivity and profit.

The character of non-corporate jobs has also been altered. The corporate ethos has permeated small enterprises.[21] Those who are self-employed or run their own businesses are taught that they must keep growing, for to stand still is to be uncompetitive. The same is true in the public service, where the ethos of service is unfashionable and where constant change is promoted. There is no such thing as recognizing "good enough", or accepting that it marks a high standard.

Work has also become the main resource for creating identity and social inclusion in the western world. But this situation is hierarchical. Creative and rewarding paid work is available to very narrow sectors of the population, and even then most of that work has been directed towards empty and anti-social ends.[22]

When we are among those contributing to growth by our production and our work, our personal lives tend to "grow" in tandem with the economy. We experience personal overload and fatigue. Concerns about care arise for children, our own health, our personal well-being and each other. Yet, in order to be successful within the growth-based mindset, we have to repress a sense that all is not as it should be. The nuclear family and intimate relations become the shock absorbers of stresses created by the demands of job-based lifestyles. The busyness and rushed nature of everyday activities often require that we become "emotional Spartans".[23] We are required to cultivate social and emotional minimalism. In other words, we have to avoid looking too closely at the contradictions in our lifestyles. We have to engage in denial about the consequences that work-oriented lifestyles have on our health, our close relationships and our relationships to people all over the world. We also have to repress our gut feelings that so much of what the system requires of us is wrong. We stop questioning, for the most part, in a struggle to get by. Such repression and absence of questioning are essential if growth is to continue unchecked.

Suppressing contradictions is bad for our mental health, and depression is a rapidly growing illness. Psychological and spiritual diseases of affluence are also on the rise. On one hand we have the limited value of material wealth, even as we are encouraged to accumulate money and possessions. On the other hand, many feel trapped in a system that appears unchangeable.

Personal escape is a means by which some try to overcome the stresses of their jobs or to bury contradictions. One can take a holiday, or drugs, or alcohol, for example. In general, it is initially easier for the cash-rich to indulge in personal escape. But personal escape becomes harder to find. We become addicted and require greater doses of whatever gives us relief. Even for the rich, things like clean air are becoming rarer; if, for example, your child suffers from asthma caused by air pollution it is harder to leave it behind, as the rich once did, although the poor rarely had that choice. The number of untouched places in the world is diminishing fast; it becomes increasingly difficult to escape the consequences of pollution and climate change. Finding an untouched, pristine holiday destination is becoming more and more difficult.

Insecurity becomes endemic

The growth-oriented system is set up so that everybody experiences insecurity to varying degrees, depending on where one lives in the world. We have already seen that millions live outside the growth system and are vulnerable to displacement from their land when it is required for raw materials. They know desperate insecurity. Internationally, security takes the form of control and containment, attacking the symptoms and keeping a lid on problems of poverty and marginalization in both the majority and the minority worlds, rather than tackling the causes of the disease.[24] However, this modern drive for control is very selective; it has failed to control destruction of eco-systems and associated global warming, the exploitation of people and animals and the depletion of natural resources.

In the minority world too, affluence brings no guarantee of security. Workers never know when their jobs will go. Trades unions may fight these developments but as long as they remain caught up in the growth mindset, they are only tinkering within the system. The minimum wage, which is certainly a morally well motivated demand and, on the face of it, good for workers, is in reality an engine of growth (see more on this in Chapter 4).

It is also increasingly difficult for those who are doing well in the short term to be truly secure. It is hard to escape the consequences of poverty, such as increased unrest stemming from migration and latent racism. The affluent can retreat into high-security gated communities or even into high-security states, but these cannot hold the security forever. True security arises from stability and equality. Fences and security guards are only a stopgap that treats symptoms rather than causes.

Under such a system, we are more likely to compete than to cooperate, although we are biologically capable of both modes of behavior. The system encourages greed and selfishness. We become less likely to have feeling and compassion for other sentient beings, and more likely to be aggressive towards them. In affluent countries, we may try to "stay ahead" if we can afford it, by defensive spending. Out of insecurity we may even try genetic engineering so that our children can compete with "the best".[25] The message is that everyone has an equal chance, if they read the market correctly and participate as workers (by producing and earning) and as consumers (by borrowing and spending).

Groups can also be aggressive towards neighboring groups when the natural resources that sustain them are threatened or destroyed by industrialization and globalization. Depending on where you live in the world, you may be invaded, your country may go to war, or you may find yourself a victim of attacks such as those in London, Madrid or New York.

The oil and gas dependency associated with growth economies means that governments in low-resource countries have to deal with resource-rich countries, whatever the latters' records on democracy and human rights. The huge rises in oil prices in recent times have led to deteriorating governance standards, restrictions on media and the judiciary, and rising corruption in all four energy-rich countries of the former Soviet Union: Russia, Turkmenistan, Kazakhstan and Azerbaijan.[26]

Food insecurity has been recognized only very recently. Industrialized agriculture, which supplies much of the world's food, relies on oil for fertilizers and for transport. But as climate change and oil scarcity really bite, it cannot continue its output and the transport of food all over the world will cease. Affluent countries will not have food coming in from distant places, yet they have for the most part consistently ignored the desirability of being self-reliant in food (see Chapter 3).

Escaping before the crash

Growth economics is not capable of slowing down. If it does, it will plunge into depression. It has to keep going in order to survive, so it overrides moral and ecological sensibilities. Like a vessel or a bicycle that is unstable when at rest, the system keeps going for the short term, due to momentum. But it cannot keep up this momentum indefinitely because the natural systems that provide its energy will collapse. If we continue to promote indiscriminate growth, crashes are always likely, especially as global warming really bites, along with the destruction of eco-systems, food insecurity and the dwindling of fossil fuels, particularly oil.

Tragedy is not the theme of this book. The good news is that there is still time to draw back from a general crash of natural systems if we adopt a global philosophy of *enough*. We need great energy to change the mindset that promotes growth, but it can be done. Moreover, the change we need is not about going back to a pre-modern way of life. Nostalgia for the past is not going to create positive futures.

The only viable alternative that will slow the train and avoid the crash is a change of heart about the god of growth. That is not to say that growth should not sometimes happen. Some kinds of economic growth *can* actually reduce resource use and pollution. Recycling industries, small-scale local agriculture carried out in ecologically sensitive ways, health services, banking and insurance, some forms of energy production and development of appropriate technologies are ecologically sound and socially benign but can still increase GDP. With sufficient eco-friendly enterprises growth can be beneficial, but beneficial growth would be very diverse and very different from the present uniform and unrestrained type of growth.

Enough supplies resources to support the change of heart we need and the practices to accompany it. Using a philosophy and practice of *enough* we can achieve a sustainable retreat for everybody in regard to global warming, climate security and social justice. With major changes to our worldview, the metaphorical train could be brought under control and slowed down to a manageable pace. We could live well without relying on exponential economic growth. But it requires both public and personal policies very different from those cultivated in the current culture. That is where the rest of the book takes us.

Beware, however. The concept of *enough* is so different from our current dominant worldview that it is often seen as an unfair critique of everything we are and everything we do in modern societies, organized as they are around unregulated economic growth. Thus, policies and practices based on *enough* often evoke defensive reactions, which include: *enough* is for losers, it will bring about recession, it is about mediocrity, it is the enemy of excellence or it will destroy our standard of living.

In spite of all these objections, *enough* needs to be part of our evolutionary strategy, as humans. We can choose to evolve in a much more complex and satisfactory way than this endless adaptation to the demands of a global growth economy, which is wringing the life out of people and the planet. We can participate in the development of our moral and ecological understanding.

We can evolve in qualitative terms rather than in measurable outputs. In a crash situation, social, job, food and cash shortages could activate latent racism and other forms of violence. There is also the possibility that it will bring out the best in people and encourage co-operation. But we ought to start co-operating now and developing viable worldwide choices before it is too late.

CHAPTER 3

SUICIDAL AGRICULTURE

Everybody eats. Food is central to who we are and essential to our security. Its importance to life cannot be overstated: we cannot live without food and if we were to do nothing else, we should examine its supply and its quality. Our food comes from farming: arable (growing grains), horticultural (vegetables and herbs) and pastoral (animal husbandry). Together, these are known as agriculture. We are intellectually deskilled if we fail to develop knowledge about food and its sources. We are practically deskilled if we cannot cook or grow food. Yet in affluent societies we have largely ceded this control to a small number of people whose chief concern is profit rather than feeding people. And in handing over responsibility, we have lost any sense of what a society would look like if it really cared about food quality, sound nutrition and food security (see Chapter 6 for more on this).

In affluent countries we have, until very recently, taken food supplies for granted. Even now, few realize how precarious our supplies are. We assume that food shortages happen only in drought or war-torn countries far away, when in reality our own sources of food could dry up at any time. Many affluent countries import most of their food. In Britain in 2000 during the fuel shortages, when hauliers of food had trouble getting around the place, there was only four and a half days' supply of food on the supermarket shelves.

I didn't want to write this chapter, because it is another one on the downsides of unregulated economic growth. I wanted to concentrate on the contents of Chapter 6, which is about real possibilities for a positive food future. But as I worked on ideas about Intelligent Agriculture, I realized I couldn't do it without sketching its suicidal opposite first. So this chapter sets out the reasons why we so badly need Intelligent Agriculture.

Ignoring *enough* in agriculture is probably the single most disastrous choice that humans have made. The drive in recent times has been to make agriculture "a business like any other", to transform it from agriculture to "agribusiness" and "food production". Policy tries to force farmers to conform to one reality only: that of cash. In order to generate maximum cash they have to aim for maximum yields from plants and animals. This means industrializing and chemicalizing an activity that is best carried out at a craft or artisan level. Yet, many of us take the industrial system so much for granted that it is now commonly called "conventional" agriculture.

In industrial farming, economies of scale operate the same as they do in other growth-oriented enterprises (see Chapter 2). For farmers, this means substituting technology and machinery for skilled human labor. Paying off the cost of the technology and machinery reduces profit margins so the farmer steps up production in order to sell more commodities, be they be eggs, pigs, chickens, liters of milk, or other "units of production". The logic is that one can make a profit by selling more low-margin goods. The pressure is then constantly on the farmer to grow the business and sell ever-more units, more cheaply, or be swamped by a bigger competitor who can sell even more goods, at an even lower shelf-price. This is called being "productive", and it is the only way to meet costs in this industrial model of farming (or any other business).

Modern industrial-scale agriculture produces food that, until very recently, has been inexpensive to purchase, but relatively expense in terms of soil, nutrition, habitats, biodiversity, animal welfare, water purity, human health and family livelihoods from family farms. It creates poverty and homelessness for millions of small farmers around the world. It is incapable of feeding the world in the long term because it is exhausting soil fertility without replenishing it. Its greenhouse gas emissions (carbon, methane and nitrous oxide) are major contributors to global warming and resulting climate change, drought and desertification.

Cash-driven, so called "progressive" agriculture policies have overturned earlier systems where many ordinary people were involved in complex local and small-scale growing, husbandry and food preparation. These processes existed in harmony with nature and produced reliable yields of good quality food. Such systems still exist in many places, as we shall see in Chapter 6, but they are under pressure from policies that encourage the mass-production of food by small numbers of people. This monetarized, industrialized, modern agribusiness is most cash-efficient when carried out on a global scale. Not all countries have industrialized their agriculture to the same extent, but industrialization is the global trend.

Beginnings

Europe saw the beginnings of globalized, industrialized agriculture in 1958, with the introduction of the Common Agricultural Policy (CAP) of the Common Market (now the European Union or EU). The CAP is one model of industrializing farming and the one on which I focus most in what follows. The USA also developed industrialized and chemicalized methods of agriculture after the Second World War, as did the state farms under Stalin in the USSR and in Israel. While details of the EU's CAP may differ from other policies, it represents a questionable modernist approach to farming and food.

The CAP came about in a Europe still recovering from World War Two and it aimed to increase productivity from land, ensure a fair standard of living for those working in agriculture, stabilize agricultural markets, secure food supplies and ensure that consumers paid fair prices for agricultural products.[1] It also brought a new ideology of farming, which encouraged farming communities to be more "modern" and more profit-oriented.[2] Peasant farming was discouraged under the CAP because it was considered backward and farmers were encouraged to move away from traditional mixed farming. They were encouraged to produce the maximum yield from their farms even if the food was not needed locally or in another part of the EU. The EU would buy surpluses at a fixed price. Surplus food went into the infamous wine and milk lakes and the butter and meat-mountains of the 1980s. Dumping of food surpluses became endemic to the system. African farmers frequently found that they could not compete with the goods supplied at knock-down prices from the food mountains and lakes of Europe and quickly they went out of business.

EU farmers were also guaranteed a price in the form of subsidies if they exported their goods. CAP subsidies to the European sugar industry were huge until recently (71 per cent of funds in 1991, for example).[3] In Europe, sugar comes from sugar beet, which is an annual crop that cannot be produced as cheaply as perennial sugar cane in the tropics. CAP subsidies made it possible to produce European sugar cheaply, however, and it was sold so cheaply on world markets that the sugar industries of Brazil and several Caribbean countries were destroyed.

Many of those who developed and promoted industrialized agriculture had good motives: they wanted to provide food security and a decent income for farmers. But they relied on a modernist science that operated without any sense of *enough*; they thought they could do things better than nature and the "backward" traditional mixed farms. Instead, they aimed for maximum yield from the soil and from animals, rather than reliable sufficient yields. This brought about serious long-term damage to the natural and human ecosystems on which all agriculture depends.

In the USA the introduction of industrialization in agriculture was certainly part of a government drive to control small farmers. It was a means to deliberately force many of them off the land and to favor the creation of large, high-yield farms. Smaller farmers had traditionally been nonconformists and had created alliances with the labor movement in an effort to control the expansion and power of corporations.[4]

Whether well intentioned or anti-farmer, the modernist policies of industrializing agriculture in the end came to reflect the interests of big growers, food processors and buyers of grain. They never favored the interests of family farms. Nevertheless, the rhetoric of competitiveness and free trade persuaded many smaller farmers that they had no choice but to go into agribusiness, even though they are thoroughly disadvantaged within that system. The logic behind industrial agriculture is that it should pursue money, rather than try to establish self-reliance in food for a country or region. As an illustration of such logic, the big growers and buyers are now turning to biofuels, where the objective is the production of fuel for cars instead of food for people. They turn to whatever is currently most profitable in order to provide maximum profit for shareholders. But this links food and fuel prices and whenever fuel prices are high, the price of food rises also.

Britain and the US are currently the most industrialized countries, with about 1 per cent of their workforces on the land. Countries with the fewest farmers are deemed to be the most "advanced". Britain in 1900 had 40 per cent of its people farming, and after World War Two, about 20 per cent.[5] The start of this process can be seen now in states that have recently joined the EU, such as Romania and Hungary.

At about the same time as the industrialization of farming began, there was a parallel development called the Green Revolution in "underdeveloped" countries. But, the term "green" here is a misnomer; the Green Revolution introduced "improved" high-yield crops, which were more responsive than older varieties to petrochemical fertilizers. Within a decade, this resulted in huge production of new strains of wheat and rice in India, Pakistan and other Asian countries.[6]

The biological risks of industrializing agriculture

It is often suggested that we cannot feed the world's population without intensive, chemically dependent and industrialized agriculture. But the opposite is the case. Such methods eventually deplete the soil so the yield drops or is not reliable. Soil requires ever-increasing amounts of nitrogen fertilizer. This is a by-product of petrol and has to be chemically produced in factories and transported to farms, where it is then applied in a blanket manner and usually in quantities that are greater than required. The plants do not take up all the nitrogen sprayed onto them, so it runs off into water courses and eventually gets into our drinking water. Some of it is also lost into the atmosphere as nitrous oxide, which is a greenhouse gas that contributes to global warming.

Traditional mixed methods produce apparently lower yields. In fact, their yields are much more reliable and they are more efficient than industrial methods, given that the inputs are much less: they don't rely on petrol-based fertilizers and long-distance transport. It takes 400 gallons of diesel to produce, process and distribute one year's worth of food for an average US citizen under industrial methods.[7]

Industrial agriculture has also become an addictive system; it destroys the health of the soil, the soil cannot then support healthy crops, and requires ever-escalating quantities of fertilizers, pesticides and fuel. When monocultures of grain or animals are cultivated they produce huge quantities of food in one place, which cannot be consumed there. The food then has to be distributed around the world or the system cannot survive. This is another addictive trait.

Modern large-scale farming depends on being able to grow crops as monocultures, in other words, acres and acres of the same crop with no variety (as with wheat in the east of England, and corn (maize) in the USA). The horticulture and occasional animals that once fitted in around the main crops on mixed farms have to go because they get in the way of the huge machines used for tilling and harvesting. Hedgerows are taken out, wildlife suffers and the land is more exposed to eroding winds.

Monocultures cause the extinction of other plants. In turn, this gives rise to nutritional deficiencies. One example is lack of vitamin A, which according to the World Health Organization is currently the cause of blindness in 40 million children. Vitamin A occurs in the body when we consume enough carotene. Traditional diets make it very easy to get enough carotene. It is found in many green vegetables, in carrots and in several plants that grow extremely easily in the tropics, such as mango and papaya. Yet, in many tropical areas these plants have been wiped out due to monocultures and the result is blindness. Scientists who support industrial agriculturalists have responded by developing genetically modified rice that contains carotene in order to combat the problem.[8]

Monocultures are also subject to pests and disease because growing the same hybridized crop over one large area is far removed from the diversity of plants that exists in nature. When diversity disappears so also do the natural predators of pests and preventers of disease. A small number of workers oversee the crops in large-scale operations and they do not have the time or the training to examine every plant and determine what it needs. Science and technology are called on for blanket measures to treat problems that arise when natural systems are disrupted. With crops, this usually involves routine extensive spraying programs, as a preventive measure. But resistance to pesticides develops and new ones are required. A second response to the vulnerability of monocultures is to develop genetically modified crops that resist pests and diseases. But this is carried out without knowledge of the long-term consequences to nature and to human health of such modified organisms. Scientific research is largely financed by manufacturers of fertilizer, pesticides and genetically modified seeds.

Monocultures are also vulnerable in the face of global warming and accompanying climate change. They are not adaptable to changing conditions in the way that traditional mixed farming is. On mixed farms, if one element fails, other crops survive and can keep the farm going. In monocultures, if one crop fails, that affects an entire farm.

Intensive arable and horticultural growing often involves crops that are not native to an area, such as celery in Spain and rice in Australia. These crops rely on huge amounts of water for irrigation, and the result is depleted aquifers. Irrigation practices can also cause salination, making land unusable. As a result, cultivatable areas are shrinking. (Global warming is also responsible for the shrinking of cultivatable areas and, as we shall see, agricultural practices create the greenhouse gases that cause warming.)

Animal suffering

The story is no better when it comes to animals, especially chickens, pigs and cattle. Animals in industrialized farming are viewed as units, not sentient beings. They are kept in conditions that do not require much human attention, apart from feeding and dosing with drugs (usually done mechanically where the "operatives" just have to push a few buttons).

When animals are "grown" under industrialized conditions, without room to move or without access to sunlight or the outdoors, they are crowded and distressed. This, combined with the unnatural diets they get, makes them unable to fight off infections and disease. For example, cattle standing constantly in manure get foot rot. Intensively farmed dairy cattle suffer from hip displacement. Drugs, including antibiotics in many countries, are widely used in order to prevent and treat disease.

Confined conditions and monocultures of animals also give diseases like foot and mouth and avian flu a chance to spread. In aquaculture (fish farming), similar problems apply.

Industrialized practices also increase the chances of epidemics like bovine spongiform encephalitis (BSE). It is caused by giving cattle food made from the remains of other animals, even though cattle are naturally vegetarian. Once a disease such as BSE takes hold, it spreads, and the only way to control it is to destroy entire herds.

Industrialization has also spread to butchering. Small slaughterhouses, with creative craft butchers, have largely disappeared and those remaining are under pressure. Supermarkets want to cut shelf costs all the time in order to maximize profit to shareholders. They cut costs by getting meat from central processing plants where animals are killed and processed on assembly lines. Speeds can be as fast as 390 cows and 1,000 pigs per hour, and 25 chickens per minute. If workers do not keep up with these speeds, they are penalized. High quotas mean that workers often resort to violent measures to keep the lines running and animals are often skinned or dismembered while they are still alive. Meat produced under such conditions can become contaminated with fecal matter and other adulterants.[9]

In growth economies, there is always a rise in meat eating. It becomes a mark of progress to get away from the most common sort of healthy traditional diet, consisting mostly of whatever grains and leaves grow well in a particular area, supplemented with small amounts of meat.[10] It is very profitable for the food industry if people eat more meat. To produce meat in large quantities requires intensive rearing. Intensively produced livestock and poultry do not have access to a natural diet, so they are fed corn or soy. This fattens them quickly but produces a meat less nutritious - and actually dangerous to human health - than meat from grass-fed or natural-diet animals. It is another form of monoculture. The food industry spends a lot of money convincing consumers that meat is the best source of protein, even though we can get plenty of first-class proteins by combining various plant foods. But the planet cannot support the 55 billion animals raised each year for slaughter. It is a very poor use of natural resources to feed animals with grain when humans could live on grain directly. And the demand for large quantities of livestock food also requires monocultures of corn (maize) or soy.

Large-scale monocultures of animals also produce manure that contains hormone and antibiotic residues along with heavy metals. Runoff from the manure gets into water courses and the residues eventually show up in our drinking water. Even if runoff can be prevented, large concentrated amounts of manure cannot be absorbed by surrounding soil. Some animal manure is good for the soil, but not the huge quantities that result from industrialized pig, chicken or cattle production.

Effects on human health

Food from chemically dependent industrialized agriculture is of poor quality and low nutritional value. Industrial farming is out of touch with modern biology, which takes a much more ecological approach. Mainstream biologists long ago abandoned the practice of concentrating on the effects of a single measure such as fertilizer, taken in isolation. They also understand that we cannot get nutritious and flavorsome food from degraded soil. But agronomists in industrial farming still apply chemicals to crops in search of higher yields. Nitrogen fertilizers do not stimulate nutrient density but excess growth of sappy tissue with thin cell walls.[11] Animals fed intensively grown grain and soy do not get the nutrients they need, nor do they nourish us (humans). Their milk, meat and eggs are low in the essential fats and minerals we need for good health.

Nutritionists have now started telling us to cut down on red meat and eat more fish. But intensively farmed fish is also fed grain. In fact, naturally reared beef is better for our health than farmed salmon.[12] It all depends on the conditions under which the meat and fish are raised and central to this is their diet. The industrial food system has made high-calorie, low-nutrition food the cheapest on the supermarket shelves. It is little wonder, therefore, that many people are overfed while at the same time being undernourished, and that this problem disproportionately affects people on the lowest incomes.

Plant food, meat, milk, milk products and eggs from industrial methods fail to nourish us properly. But even worse, they actively harm us. Food coming from industrial methods contains a mixture of polyunsaturated and saturated fats, chemicals and hormones, which one would never find in nature.[13] This cocktail results from the pesticides and fertilizers for plants and the drugs and food given to livestock and poultry. This industrial-petro-chemical mixture introduces xeno-hormones, especially xeno-estrogen, into the human system ("xeno" means "foreign" or "strange"). For good health, we are supposed to have estrogen and other hormones such as testosterone and progesterone (women and men need different proportions of them), but they should be of a kind that the body produces naturally, when it is properly nourished. The foreign hormones, especially xeno-estrogen, invade the body's receptors for natural hormones and take up the spaces that should be occupied by the natural hormones. They cause estrogen dominance in both sexes.

Estrogen dominance prevents a correct hormonal balance and is responsible for a host of illnesses and syndromes seen in affluent countries. Breast and prostate cancer, allergies, fatigue, premenstrual syndrome, menopausal trauma, the growth of breasts in men, undescended testicles and infertility are just some of the conditions that can be laid at the door of the xeno-estrogens.[14] The food provided for us by industrial farming is toxic and it is shameful that this has become normalized. We accept the inevitability of the syndromes and illnesses, but, apart from natural health practitioners, medicine ignores their causes. Instead, modern medicine treats the symptoms with surgery and / or with patented (and money-making) drugs. On the one hand governments are concerned about obesity and the increase in cancer while on the other hand they encourage the industrial-ization of our food chain, which is largely responsible for the creation of the problems in the first place.

The greenhouse gas emissions

As if all this were not bad enough, modern agriculture is a major contributor to global warming, with its greenhouse-gas emissions of methane, nitrous oxide and carbon dioxide. Nitrous oxide comes from the nitrogen fertilizers and manures applied to soils. Methane from large-scale cattle operations is also signif-icant; it comes from the way food ferments in the stomachs of cattle. Grain or soy-fed cattle produce much more methane than those grass-fed in the traditional way. Ecosystem carbon dioxide is released into the atmosphere in huge quantities when native vegetation like forest is cleared in order to grow monocultures of soy and palm oil.[15] Modern agriculture is also dependent on cheap fossil fuels for heating, fertilizer, pesticides, machinery and transport. Consuming fossil fuels causes carbon-dioxide emissions.

Global warming causes climate change and this affects how food can be grown in different parts of the world: conditions are already changing and will continue to change. If we cannot halt it before it exceeds the two-degree centigrade threshold (See Chapter 4), all the accumulated wisdom that still exists concerning traditional farming methods will then be useless under these very different conditions. Thus, modern agriculture is eroding the natural systems that support it. Unfortunately, it is also making conditions difficult for more ecologically sound and sustainable types of farming.

Changes in the Common Agricultural Policy

In the EU, some changes in the CAP were introduced in the early 1990s. Smaller and poorer farms have, since 1994, been encouraged to participate in the Rural Environmental Protection Scheme (REPS). Under REPS, the EU pays farmers to follow prescribed basic measures to protect the environment. Water resources are to be protected from the pollution that results from run-off or seepage of nitrogen, phosphorous, lime, herbicides and pesticides. Grassland has to be sustainably managed, water-courses and wells have to be maintained and protected; wildlife habitats are to be protected from the effects of intensive farming, including drainage, afforestation, turf-cutting and burning. Stone walls and hedges are to be maintained. Historical and archaeo-logical features have to be preserved.[16]

Initially, this led to a two-tiered system which imposed environmental concerns on small farmers while the "productive" industrialized farms continued business as usual. In the early 1990s, however, CAP reforms also started to reduce stockpiles and surpluses. More recently subsidies for production were withdrawn (de-coupling), in order to bring internal EU markets into line with international prices. Under de-coupling, farmers will get direct subsidies based on the size of their farm, instead of subsidies for their produce. This is designed to allow prices to fall in line with demand, but without undermining farmers' liveli-hoods.[17] Payments will be contingent on good standards in respect of environment, food safety, general safety and animal welfare. There will also be an upper limit on the total subsidies paid to farmers so that the existing distortions, in which larger farmers can make massive profits from the CAP, will disappear. Savings made on subsidies will be diverted to rural development funding. Several member countries have tried to negotiate opt-out agreements to suit the demands of national farming pressure groups, which usually represent the big farmers, who have industrialized their operations.

The reforms have also introduced much stricter legislation on the control of pollution, in the form of the Nitrates Directive, which is concerned with run-off from the use of nitrogen as a fertilizer. Sadly, however, the reforms have made no attempt to deal with monocultures and therefore with loss of biodiversity and soil depletion, which result in the use of fertilizer and pesticides. The reforms are essentially environmental management, or rather an attempt to limit and manage the damage caused by industrialized practices. They have little ecological sensitivity because they do not examine the whole-system effects of industrial farming. Neither do the reforms try to get more people into farming. (Chapter 6 has some suggestions for making reform much more radical and ecological in nature, for the CAP or in any other country that currently has similar policies.)

The new CAP reforms initially led to price reductions for many agricultural goods in the EU (although it is questionable how long the reductions can continue, in the face of dwindling oil supplies). Those African and Asian farmers who have managed to sell successfully within the EU are now finding that they have to further reduce their prices in order to compete with the new lower EU prices. At the lower prices, they are unable to make a profit and they have no back-up of direct subsidies, like the EU farmers do. Having gone along with the free-trade policies of the World Trade Organization (WTO) and invited majority-world farmers to compete in a world market, the EU is now making it impossible for those farmers to survive.

The social and human effects of industrial agriculture

It takes far fewer workers to run large-scale agricultural operations than to run traditional farming and associated crafts such as butchering, whether the operations involve animals or crops. So as agriculture becomes industrialized, people leave the land. Sometimes people are literally pushed off the land, as when native vegetation is cleared for large-scale operations. Outsiders, often big corporations, buy the land the people once farmed in traditional ways. Or, less dramatic but equally serious, over time, farms cannot support an entire household; family livelihoods decline. Robust rural societies disappear and rural life becomes a struggle. Given this downward spiral, young people do not want to stay in the countryside. Many have migrated to cities, but millions of small farmers in Africa, South America, India and China have resorted to suicide, and thousands in "developed" countries have also taken this route.

The displaced people generally make their way to cities. This results in increased urban dwelling and the development of suburbs around cities and towns. We have already seen this in Ireland and other parts of Europe and it is happening almost everywhere now. China, for example, is currently building 500 new cities. 2007 was the first year when over half of the world's population lived in cities. The countryside is reduced to a place where car-dependent commuters live when they are not working in the cities. When new towns and cities are not planned shanty-towns grow up around existing cities. The former rural people often find it difficult to get work in cities or have to endure exploitative working conditions. In addition, they now have to buy the food they once grew for themselves. This has knock-on negative effects on their health, as the food they buy is not as fresh or nutritious as what they used to grow.

The global nature of agri-business also means that land is used for growing food for export rather than for home needs (and this is often the case even with organically produced food). In the case of many poor countries, economic "development" is under-stood to mean that they should grow cash crops on a large scale and sell to rich countries. Costa Rica, for example, has suffered from a bilateral agreement with the USA, enforced by the WTO. As a result, Costa Rica has been forced to abandon its traditional staple crops of maize (corn) and beans in order to grow coffee for export. It sells the coffee on world markets and has to buy grain from the USA at inflated prices.[18] Further, those prices are going to get even higher because grain shortages are already appearing in the USA. Both weather and oil costs are driving down yields of corn, soy and wheat. There is also a trend in the USA to produce corn for ethanol or biodiesel because it fetches a higher price than corn sold for food, but it takes many acres out of food production. Americans are going to have trouble feeding themselves in the years ahead, and will have little surplus for export or for aid.

Despite this, policy-makers everywhere are under pressure from the WTO and the World Bank to encourage their domestic agriculturalists to become export-focused. Developing countries are "encouraged" to grow commodity crops (soy, pineapples, coffee, palm oil, peanuts, bananas, green beans, flowers or shrimps) rather than food for their people. The idea is that they sell the commodity crops for cash on the world market and use the cash to buy wheat and corn from the USA (and, increasingly, from China). These growing operations rarely bring any benefit other than low wages to local people. People working on farms often become malnourished while growing good food for export. It is a myth that if Europeans buy green beans or other fresh food from Kenya we are helping poor farmers there. Those people were put out of the global profit picture long ago.[19]

Apart from the biological consequences of large-scale monocultures, the morality of "inviting" countries to join the industrialized globalized agricultural markets is deeply questionable. The poor countries are urged to join the global market so as to get rich. But they will be able to compete in the global market only if they stay poor and continue to work for rock-bottom wages.[20] What is more, the export markets could collapse at any time, leaving those who are earning a wage from the export food business without the cash they have come to depend on, which they use to buy grain they would once have grown for themselves. And now, even the grain-exporting countries like the USA and China are experiencing shortages.

Genetically modified seeds

The industrialized system of agriculture is designed to make profits for a few. Nowhere is this more evident than in the development of genetically modified "terminator seeds". The seeds are called terminators because they give a crop, but the seeds from that crop are infertile. The farmers are persuaded that it is better to buy the modified seed in the first place because it may be more resistant to pests and diseases than their traditional varieties. This is not necessarily true, but propaganda makes it seem so. They cannot save or share seed to plant their next crop because the seed is infertile.

Even where the genetically modified seed they buy is not a terminator seed, the farmers are not allowed to save some for the next crop: legislation has been enacted to make this illegal on the grounds that the seed has been patented and is the property of the corporation that sold it to them in the first place. The aim of corporate monopoly is to make every farmer dependent on buying seeds from corporations in every planting season.[21] As well as making money for the corporations, the effect is to reduce local variety in crops and in food. This has become the norm for large-scale industrial farmers to such an extent that many no longer consider it unjust. But small farmers the world over have always used seed from one crop to plant the next. Once they get into the cycle of genetically modified seeds, this traditional wealth is denied to them.

Work and industrialized agriculture

Official development policy is that most people should work in jobs away from the land, in IT, tourism, service work or manufacturing, depending on the part of the world they live in. These jobs are supposedly more skilled than farming and contribute more to economic growth. If you grow and eat your own food you are not contributing to GDP.

Worldwide, there simply are not enough jobs in the official "high-skill" alternatives to farming. Many resort to prostitution, drug running, professional begging, scavenging or mercenary soldiering depending on where they live. A lot of people end up in jail, which is a huge and growing industry in Britain and the US. Or the displaced migrate to other parts of the world where they think they may get jobs.

Those who work in industrialized agriculture are unfortunate too, since it is deskilled and alienating work, with low pay and poor conditions. The system cannot do without labor altogether, but it uses the cheapest labor possible: immigrants, sometimes illegal, who can be fired or threatened with the law if they object to the conditions.

The work has to be over-simplified to make it do-able on a large scale and to keep it low-labor and thereby save on wages. Some workers will be exposed to pesticides, especially in countries that do not have regulations in place. According to the World Health Organization, pesticide poisoning causes 220,000 human deaths a year.[22] Others will work in animal-production "units", where the treatment of animals is degrading to the human spirit as well as bad for the animals.

The dehumanized, sometimes dangerous and out-of-touch-with-nature conditions in industrialized agriculture make most agricultural work very unattractive. Nevertheless, the false notion is cultivated for the buying public that this kind of farming is clean and sanitized and that traditional mixed farming on family farms is backward, dirty, hard and something to leave behind. So a further social and human effect of industri-alized agriculture is a rural-urban divide, where all kinds of farming are regarded as low-skill, and other "modern" or "progressive" kinds of work are seen as high-skill.

Industrialized agriculture fits with the modern view that everyone should live in a suburbanized environment, drive a car to a nice clean job and earn a salary with which to buy the food produced by a few workers pushing buttons on factory-farms. This is the modern vision of the future for humanity: as far from the land as possible. With this separation from the land, people lose much of the sense of place that contributes to diverse regional identities.[23] Food, houses, work, and landscape tend to become similar the world over, pushing people into monocultural lifestyles.

Long supply chains

Long global food chains obscure the origins of our food and the human, animal and planetary suffering. Battery farmed hens, pigs in cramped conditions, soy, palm oil, bananas, coffee, peanuts, pineapples, shrimps and salmon are all tainted with injustice and cruelty. But the consumer in the affluent world can ignore the industrialization of agriculture and its effects on people, animals and nature, because they are far from us, either shut away in production units or far away in miles.

The quality and flavor of food are also affected. Food supply chains should be as simple and direct as possible, in order to ensure freshness, safety and animal welfare. But we get jet-lagged vegetables flown in. Animals that have to travel for slaughter become distressed. And the quality of their meat deteriorates; for example, adrenalin released by stressed pigs makes their pork pale and watery.[24] Long supply chains also make it very difficult to enforce regulations regarding the safe production of food. They also create favorable conditions for the spread of diseases like foot and mouth and avian flu, which are caused by industrial rearing practices and are carried around the world when food travels.

The policy of industrialization and global movement of food creates an unstable system, which easily succumbs to disease and lack of accountability. But instead of trying to rectify this by creating stable systems, policymakers try to treat the symptoms.

They regulate on ever more minute matters (creating for example the extreme health and safety rules that annoy people so much), and introduce things like computerized traceability. Sometimes the system ties itself up in knots in the process while the regulations designed for industrial production adversely affect small traditional-style farmers and food producers because they cannot afford industrial-level safety precautions. In fact, because their operations are inherently safe, artisan producers do not need such precautions. But the bureaucracy makes no allowances for this, developed as it is to try to regulate a different, industrialized system.

Conclusion

The western-style modernization of agriculture is not actually designed to provide enough good food for everyone on the planet. It is immoral because its prime purpose is to generate profit for shareholders in large-scale agricultural operations and in the corporations that dominate the food-processing industry.[25] At the people end of the chain, in affluent countries we get obesity with hormone-imbalance and a modern type of malnourishment. Too many poor-quality calories, combined with sedentary lifestyles, lead to obesity and type-two diabetes, the affluent world's greatest killers at this time. On the other hand, we have famine, hunger and malnourishment in poor countries. The system puts cash over human, animal and planetary well-being.

The system is also unsustainable, and we need to remind ourselves what that term really means: sooner or later, it will collapse irretrievably. Industrialized, globalized agriculture cannot provide long-term food security because it flouts basic ecological and biological principles. We need the exact opposite of this system.

So-called economic experts constantly tell farmers that they need to reform and fit farming into "economic reality". But there are greater realities than the economic one, narrowly understood as the financial bottom line. There are biological, social and moral realities that will not go away: the human and animal misery, the vulnerability of the food supply and the industry's contribution to global warming. One of the justifications for industrial farming has been its capacity to produce food with a low shelf cost to consumers. But with oil shortages and resulting high fuel prices, shelf prices for food in affluent countries can no longer be kept down. For many people who are prepared to ignore the ecological and moral consequences of industrialized agriculture, rising prices may finally lead them to scrutinize and question the system.

Fortunately, there has always been a different kind of farming, which is ethically and morally sound and, in terms of total cost, gives us food that is just as affordable as food from the industrialized system. It gets less attention than and is under threat from industrialized practices. But it is experiencing a revival, and it is the subject of Chapter 6.

CHAPTER 4

REGULATING FOR FREEDOM

Global warming changes everything we know about how to "develop". The stories we have told ourselves in modern times about the meaning of progress and development have emphasized humans' independence from the earth and our capacity to pursue goals of growth, without taking the planet into account. The shadow sides of growth have been noted for some time,[1] although they have been played down in the mainstream media. But one shadow side is now particularly clear in the form of accelerated global warming. The earth probably experiences natural cyclical changes in temperature, but human activity is also increasing the rate of global warming.

Since about 2007, there has been far less general public denial of global warming than there was in the years before, even when scientists recognized that global warming was taking place. Most people now accept that the natural systems that sustain us are suffering due to overheating, and that we need to find ways to regulate human activity in order to reduce carbon emissions and thereby reduce global warming. The planet's ecosystems are forcing us to take seriously the damage we have caused.

It is essential that we do not allow crises in banks and other financial institutions to overshadow the threat posed by global warming. Global warming is quite literally destroying the earth's capacity to nourish humans and supply us with resources. It is having serious effects, both current and rapidly increasing. These effects – such as drought, flooding and the collapse of eco-systems — may seem less obviously and immediately threatening to the way we live than a collapse of financial institutions. But in the long term and the not-so-long term they are much more serious.

The planet has a finite capacity to cope with the waste gases created by human activity, especially the high-energy industries and lifestyles of growth economies. These gases stay in the atmosphere, where they form a sort of blanket over the earth, trapping heat and preventing the earth from cooling as it should. Carbon dioxide is the most serious culprit, and is produced when we burn coal, oil and gas. Other gases such as methane and nitrous oxide also play a part and we need to take measures to reduce them (see Chapter 5), but regulating carbon emissions is the most urgent task.

The essential question is how to draw all countries and all people into a process for reducing carbon emissions and preventing the situation from becoming much worse. The answer lies in creating the fairest possible legislation for reduction. Fairness in this context means applying the same rules to all countries and all individuals. The Kyoto protocol is the best-known global attempt to regulate carbon emissions. It has been rejected by the USA and Australia on the grounds that it would hamper their economic growth, while it is also ignored by China and India. (The USA may change this policy under President Obama.)

Poorer African countries have also objected to entering a regulation agreement such as the Kyoto protocol, because it would restrict their freedom to pursue economic growth in the ways that the so-called "developed" countries have done. It would, in effect, make them suffer for the excesses of those who have been before them in the growth race. It makes no provision for fairness and a just apportioning of resources in responding to global warming.

Each of these countries' objections is based on a sound human reaction to regulation for any emergency: when we try to tackle a problem, the rules must be the same for everyone. Aubrey Meyer and a number of independent thinkers have combined good science (for reduction of global warming) with democracy, creativity and imagination (for a fair process) and have developed a framework called Contraction and Convergence,[2] in which everyone would play by the same rules. It is very radical in its fairness, and perhaps this is why it has not received the support it deserves in the minority affluent world. But it has some influential supporters in the affluent world, including Angela Merkel, the German chancellor, Hillary Benn, the British Environment Secretary, the Royal Commission on Environmental Pollution and many Green parties.[3] It has also attracted "eclectic support" from the European Parliament, the Red Cross and some business and insurance-industry leaders.[4]

China, India and many African countries support the idea of equal per capita allocation of global commons resources, which is the basis of the justice of Contraction and Convergence.[5] The Contraction and Convergence framework is essentially about fairly apportioning everyone's entitlements to a scarce resource. It is about sharing what we all need, but don't have much of, namely the capacity to emit carbon-dioxide.

We need to imagine the consequences of *not* reducing carbon emissions and ask what will happen if we allow the earth's temperatures to rise over a crucial two-degree threshold. It is easy to portray as attractive a rise in overall temperatures in the temperate zones: they would have a warmer and more pleasant climate. But even that approach ignores the dangers from flooding and storms in those zones, which we are already seeing at this time. What is more, emphasizing the pleasant effects for temperate zones downplays the devastating effects on other parts of the world: drought, flooding and the destruction of eco-systems essential for life.

We also need to imagine the consequences of introducing reduction measures without the ingredient of fairness. We will see higher energy prices, without any extra income to compensate for them; profits for large corporations while ordinary citizens suffer and dissent from those countries which have not been responsible for excess emissions in the past.

Accepted: the need to reduce and regulate carbon emissions

A 90 per cent reduction in global carbon emissions over the next twenty-five to fifty years will keep us under a dangerous two degree Centigrade limit.[6] We could reduce globally by 10 per cent per year, over the next twenty-five years.[7] The Kyoto protocol proposes a 60 per cent global reduction. But a 90 per cent reduction is a much better bet to keep us under the two-degree ceiling.

If the world's temperature rises more than two degrees over pre-industrial temperatures, we are in severe trouble. They have already risen a third of this two degrees, and will certainly rise a further third, due to the emissions we have already made, but which have not yet taken effect. We must stop them rising that last third. Although it is not a perfect target, a two-degree rise is a threshold that we cannot exceed without the following consequences: more global water shortages; failure in agricultural systems, including those of the world's largest exporters of food (USA and China); the loss of the world's most diverse ecosystems including the Amazon rainforests and the coral reefs; and twelve metre rises in sea levels with attendant flooding.[8]

In order to achieve a 90 per cent reduction we need to move gradually towards identical emissions across the world's population of less than 1.5 tons per person. In Britain the annual average emission per person is now close to 11 tons. In Ireland it is 17 tons with most of this coming from transport. In China, it is 4 tons, in India, it is 1.8, while in Africa, the average over all countries is less than one ton per person.[9] Clearly, some countries need to contract more than others.[10] Those that are under the target can actually continue to engage in activities that increase emissions, should they choose to do so.

The reduction we need to make is referred to as Contraction. Contraction is a quantitative dimension of *enough*; we can measure the required reduction in our carbon emissions in order to stay – if not completely unaffected, since many changes cannot be halted – at least under that dangerous two-degree threshold.

Needed: a fair process for regulation

Contraction or reduction represents the substance of the story about how to save the planet from further warming: it is part of a coping strategy that we need at this time. Equally important is a fair process or method, designed in a way that draws in all countries and all individuals to participate in the strategies for reduction. It needs to ensure maximum benefit from carbon reduction for the greatest numbers of people all over the world. A process has already been worked out which is in accord with the attitude of *enough*: it is fair, just, and morally sound; it is also simple, ecological and aesthetic. The framework calls this process Convergence.

Global Convergence has two strands: first, that every country participates in an international reduction agreement; second, that the cuts give equal emission rights to every citizen in the world. The two strands are essential and mutually reinforcing because the distribution of equal emission rights to every citizen is what makes the process fair. This fairness is the carrot that can encourage every country to participate. It could draw in those countries currently not participating in the Kyoto Protocol (Australia, India, China and USA, for example).

The global commons

As citizens of the globe, we all have equal rights to "dump" our waste gas emissions in the atmosphere. The atmosphere is part of the global commons;[11] it is a resource (like air, water and soil) that belongs to everyone, insofar as it can be said to belong to anyone at all. With Convergence, every citizen in the world gets an equal quota of carbon-dumping entitlement. One could of course argue that no citizen has the right to dump anything. But we have been dumping for a long time, and it would seem impossible to stop all dumping completely; that situation might come about eventually, however, after a period of drastically reduced dumping brought about by Contraction and Convergence.

Each person can use their quota in total or trade it in a legitimate worldwide carbon market. So to start with, those who are thrifty with their emissions will be able to sell their quota – or part of it – to those who can afford to buy extra in order to do carbon-heavy activities. Governments, corporations and industries that need to make a lot of carbon emissions will be able to buy on that market also.

If individual citizens each get the share that is theirs by right, trading will provide some income to offset the higher costs of energy that will accompany carbon reduction. Any form of reduction of carbon emissions is going to increase the price of energy, no matter what process is used. For that reason, a lot of people still resist the idea of reduction despite evidence on global warming. A process that gives people extra income from trading would also help to make emissions reduction more popular. Extra income would also help those who are poor, because they for the most part live in badly insulated homes and have to spend a large percentage of their incomes on heating. Extra income for them, particularly if combined with support from government for improving insulation, would be particularly welcome.

With Convergence in place, things change immediately. Government does not have to regulate carbon emissions any further, beyond deciding the quota for each person. Nobody is monitored minutely regarding their carbon emissions, or forced to do anything they do not want. We can all live as we please, as long as it is within our carbon ration. We can buy or sell carbon allowances depending on whether we are frugal or profligate. If you are frugal with your allowance, you have an opportunity to make extra income from selling the unwanted part of your ration. If you want to run a haulage company, take flights, drive long journeys alone in a big car, or light up your house at Christmas you can buy surplus carbon quotas and engage in your chosen activity, all within the rules. The cost of buying surplus will of course rise steadily as each person's ration becomes smaller from year to year.

Contraction and Convergence offers a radical blend of libertarianism and regulation.[12] In the present political climate in affluent societies it would be regarded as a violation of human rights, not to mention very difficult to achieve, if governments were to monitor the energy use and emissions of airlines, haulage companies or individuals in their homes. But with quotas and trading everyone is free to travel by air, to transport goods by air or road or to expend energy as they please, as long as they do it within their carbon quota. If they cannot do it within their quota, they have the option of buying surplus from other people. It would make travel more expensive, but the price would be more representative of the ecological cost.

The immediate reaction to this is usually that the framework gives an advantage to those who have money, because they can buy quotas, continue to drive a car or fly, while the poor are able to sell their quotas and walk or use public transport. In the beginning, this probably would be the most likely scenario. The same would also be the case, however, if we introduced taxes, but with taxes there would be no prospect of a leveling-out of the advantages over time. The significant difference with Contraction and Convergence is that the poor, or those who did not want to fly or drive, would get money in exchange for their quotas. Taxation would not give them extra money in their pockets. They could use the extra money from quota-trading as they pleased, but most importantly it would be available for meeting more easily the increased costs of essential energy for heating homes.

There would be real incentives for individuals and corporations to develop carbon-neutral energy systems, goods and services; these would automatically have market advantage, because the trading system would encourage people always to look for the most energy-efficient equipment or option. By choosing energy efficiency, consumers would save on carbon emissions, thus having more of their quotas to sell. Public transport, especially if carbon-efficient (powered with electricity from solar, hydro or wind sources), would also have a market advantage. Government would not have to legislate to favor low-carbon goods and services.

The transport of goods around the globe in the way we know it now would be much more expensive because it would have to include the price of purchasing carbon quotas. Sailing and canal transport might have a renaissance. Supermarkets would change radically because it would not be possible to continue to transport fresh goods in the way that supermarkets now rely on. Nor would we be able to drive to supermarkets regularly in the way we do now.[13] They are, in any case, hugely wasteful of energy, for heating, refrigeration and lighting. If they wanted to continue to operate as they do now, supermarkets would have to buy massive amounts of quotas, and the price of these would affect their profits. So they might find more efficient ways to operate, by buying more local food and storing it in warehouses that do not need so much heat and light. They might promote internet shopping, allowing customers to choose and order food without having to travel, and then delivering food to homes by carbon-efficient transport.[14]

If the global transport of goods, especially of out-of season fresh food, is restricted, then locally produced goods have an advantage. This will encourage local business, especially farming, to provide quality food, ensuring variety and freshness. These are some likely outcomes in a chain reaction to reduction, quotas and trading. There would probably be many other outcomes that cannot be predicted from where we stand at this time.

Individuals first: why the framework gives quotas to people not government

The Contraction and Convergence framework treats the carbon quota as part of every person's human rights. The global commons belongs to all of us and any dividend from it should come directly to individuals, not through governments or corporations. Giving it to governments allows any government anywhere the chance to pilfer quotas that belong by right to citizens.[15] We must not think, as many of us do in affluent societies, that our governments are invariably clean and African governments are corrupt. Already, the dimension of fairness is missing from the current attempts by the EU to meet its Kyoto reduction targets.

The European Commission has accepted the idea of reduction and is using an Emissions Trading Scheme (ETS) for putting it into place. Permits have been issued to companies creating large amounts of emissions, such as cement factories, electricity generators, glass, brick, paper and steel plants. (Aviation may be brought into the process in 2010.) But this scheme is unfair because the large energy users get their licenses to emit (currently worth 170 euro billion in Europe) for free, yet they increase the price they charge to their customers, the general public, in order to make profit for their shareholders.[16] This makes energy more expensive, which particularly affects the poor. The scheme has nothing built into it to compensate buyers for higher prices. Thus, the good aspects of ETS are too easily overlooked, because of justifiable concerns about high energy prices, fuel poverty, and the possibility of vulnerable older people dying of hypothermia.[17]

Giving dumping entitlements to large enterprises, as the EU is doing now, is appropriating the global commons, something that belongs to all, and allowing a few to make a profit from it. Having set a safe limit for global carbon emissions, we must then, in the interests of fairness, give everyone the same entitlement to emit.

The ETS is also very cumbersome because those companies receive their permits well after the energy they use has entered the EU economy.

This means that their 11,500 installations have to be assessed and audited. This takes a lot of legal, accounting and administrative resources, and yet the ETS covers only 45 per cent of the EU's emissions. It would have been much better and simpler to have imposed the system right upstream ... this would have meant that monitoring would be required only for coal, gas and oil producers within the EU and those importing those fuels, perhaps 200 firms in all.[18]

It would be much simpler to administer an upstream system such as Contraction and Convergence.

It would be relatively easy to set up a system for issuing quotas to citizens, and for trading them. Everyone would be issued with something like a swipe card, and could trade at their bank or post office. Governments and corporations would then acquire through the banks or post offices enough emissions entitlements to conduct their businesses. An incentive would exist from the start for them to cut carbon emissions in order to keep their costs down. They would of course add the extra cost of acquiring the carbon quotas they needed to the sale price of any goods and services. But they would be giving us money in the first place, by trading, and this would help to meet the higher prices. We would not all be forced to become traders, but there would be an incentive to trade.

The practicalities of a fair system

The Contraction and Convergence system would mean that people would have to be registered. In affluent countries this would be relatively easy. We have got used to debit, credit and charge cards, and many use supermarket loyalty cards. But, of the six billion people on the planet, most have never seen such cards. Many are not registered anywhere, even to vote. They do not officially exist. There would have to be a drive to register everybody and this would be quite a task. But one advantage for those currently unregistered would be the receipt of a small amount of money from trading their carbon quotas. Currently, too, unregistered people cannot secure loans for enterprises. Registered, and having an official entitlement to part of the earth's resources (the atmosphere), they would find it easier.[19]

Registration and trading would also create a type of Citizens' Income. Some of this would have to be used to pay for more expensive fuel and energy, especially in countries that are currently heavy carbon-users. But the carbon-thrifty could have a surplus which would allow them some extra financial freedom, perhaps to do less paid work. Working less for pay in turn reduces the amount of consumption; the more we work, the more we spend on consumer goods and services that harm the environment. And the availability of even small amounts of cash also allows for developing entrepreneurial economic activities of a kind we cannot predict. We have seen this already when the Grameen Bank issued micro-credit to very poor women in Bangladesh.[20] (The subject of a Citizens' Income is developed more fully in Chapter 5.)

With tradable carbon quotas as a source of income, there is effectively a new currency alongside money. Its units have been referred to as EBCUs (emissions-backed currency units) and icecaps, although the name hardly matters.[21] Whatever we call them, they help us to re-define wealth.

Africa, which emits hardly any carbon compared with OECD and economically similar countries would now have a massive surplus of quotas. This new form of wealth could be turned into financial wealth by trading in surpluses. Provided the essential element of quotas going directly to individual citizens was in place, everyone would be able to trade their excess carbon quotas, creating income for all. This would allow African economies to develop and prosper, but in uniquely African ways, and without the "structural adjustments" currently forced on them, such as building roads, or developing industrialized farming, both of which are aimed at supporting export markets.[22] Intelligent, vibrant, ecologically sound local economic systems would have a chance to evolve. Diverse as they would undoubtedly be, such schemes would probably also be people-intensive, because only local self-management can possibly harness the complex productivity of any particular area.[23]

Why tradable individual quotas are better than other options for reduction

The other solutions proposed to the global warming problem are more familiar. They include carbon taxes, targeting individual behavior and encouraging people to reduce their emissions voluntarily. I take a look at each one of those options, in the sections that follow. I do not discuss nuclear power or biofuels, which are also often proposed. We have not found a way to store nuclear waste safely, and in addition to that, extracting uranium to fuel nuclear stations is itself a carbon-heavy activity. Biofuels have a potential value but not when they are grown as monocultures that take up valuable land that should be used for food. There is some place for them in mixed farms, grown in small amounts, but not much research has been carried out into this option. (See a little more on biofuels in Chapters 3 and 6)

Quotas are better than carbon taxes

Okay, people say, we need to reduce carbon emissions; we accept that. But why not apply carbon taxes instead? Taxation is a more familiar idea, and that is probably why it comes to mind so readily as a response. But taxation immediately increases prices without providing extra income to compensate as quota-trading would. Even if we do not increase taxation overall, but substitute carbon taxes for taxes on income and savings,[24] taxation still allows those with higher incomes to use up scarce resources and to pollute, simply because they have the money to do so.[25] Another problem with taxation is that a tax rate that is successful during a time of strong economic growth will be too harsh when the economy slows.[26]

In a quota system, monetary wealth does not give one the same kind of advantage. Of course, having money does allow you to buy excess from others. However, such trading puts money into the pockets of ordinary people, who can manage their own quotas, and not into the coffers of a government or corporation.

Quotas are also simpler. Taxation can be made fair, by organizing a system of rebates for the less well off, but this is complex and uses up valuable administration time. It can be difficult to understand and it is open to fraud. Although we are used to taxes such as income tax, most of us do not fully understand tax systems. Taxation also has uneven effects. With quotas, it is clear exactly what carbon savings will be made.[27]

The simplicity of quotas makes them easy for everybody to understand and straightforward and cheaper to administer. The justice of a quota system is clear to all, and this makes it more likely that people will accept it if governments propose it. Most importantly, however, sharing, quotas and their implicit fairness promote the sense that we are all in this together. Contraction and Convergence as an overall approach has a much better moral basis than taxation.

Quotas are better than targeting individual carbon emissions

Targeting individual citizens, to encourage them to change their behavior, always has uneven effects. We have seen this with antismoking campaigns. Some respond, some don't, even though the behavior is proven to be harmful. In an emergency such as we have, how should we deal with those who don't respond to campaigns to reduce their personal carbon emissions? Without quotas, the options are limited: ignore them and let them continue to live in ways that are literally endangering the future for all of us or, on the other hand, regulate every aspect of people's lives. In this latter scenario, government could effectively come into your home and see if you turn off the lights at night, or waste hot water. Inspectors could carry out any number of checks. This of course would be almost impossible to police effectively and fairly. It would also be highly undesirable, even if it were possible. People rightly object to the idea of the "nanny state". Nobody wants to be monitored all the time.

With quotas, there is no need for intrusive monitoring: everybody is contributing to and participating in the process of carbon reduction because everyone has the same carbon resources to start with. Quotas and legitimate trading – as well as having the moral edge – also have the political edge because they mean that everybody in society is operating according to the same rules. Fairness like this is a huge strategic advantage for any policy.

Quotas create equity

Quotas create equity by means of pre-distribution: the dumping capacity for carbon is calculated in a way that provides security and safe limits for all; then the available amount is shared equally among all individuals. It is like turning a tap off at the mains, then issuing a daily water ration to a household. The members cannot let the tap run all day, but they have plenty for their needs, maybe even a bit more than they want to use, and they decide for themselves how to use what they have.

Carbon quotas are an example of how policy can help to establish safe limits so that everyone can enjoy security. It would be wrong to imply that issuing quotas to meet carbon reduction targets will not mean some big changes; affluent countries' high-energy way of life, based on fossil fuels, will certainly have to be modified. But meeting reduction targets by any of the other means is also going to mean big changes. Using alternative sources of energy may allay some of the worst effects, but whatever we do, energy-based items will undoubtedly increase in price; people will spend a larger percentage of their income on electricity, fuel and food than they do now. They will not have so much disposable income to spend on flying, plastics, or disposable items. It will make us truly materialistic, in the sense that we will value material goods, the more durable the better, and we will conserve and re-use them so that they are not such an environmental problem.[28] This will happen, no matter what steps are taken to deal with global warming. But with quotas and trading in place, people will have some extra money, to offset higher prices. There will also be opportunities for innovative and creative carbon-neutral goods and services since they will have a market advantage.

We probably will never leave behind altogether the symbolic values that currently drive a lot of consumption. Many of us attempt to distinguish ourselves from others or to create an identity, by buying things that are more expensive or more exclusive than what others have. In reality, however, much of what is available in affluent consumer societies society has the effect of making us the same as others. We will all have to find other ways to achieve a unique identity, independent from the kind of carbon-heavy consumption that many now engage in.[29] Most importantly, equity is built into the quota system right from the start.

Quotas enhance quality of life

The discipline and huge changes required are the first things most people see when they consider Contraction and

Convergence. Our imaginations let us down when it comes to seeing the framework's potential for better ways to live. We should not sugar the pill about the changes in lifestyle that any form of quotas will require. For example, the effects of carbon rationing on private transport will certainly include less private car use, but this will reduce pollution and congestion. Less congestion will mean that buses can operate according to schedule and be more reliable. It will also create an environment more conducive to walking and cycling.

Increased cycling and walking, as part of everyday life, will alleviate diseases of affluence such as obesity and type-two diabetes (a form of diabetes caused by sedentary lifestyles and poor-quality high-calorie food, and currently the biggest killer in the world).[30] It will also help with quality of life. If you walk or cycle as part of daily life, as well as saving carbon and getting exercise, you meet people on the way. If you don't know them already, you will get to know them if you meet them regularly. You don't have to become best friends, just recognize and greet each other. This is good for well-being; it gives a sense of belonging and trust, which are essential to happiness. These social benefits and physical health effects are "stacking functions" that occur in any ecologically healthy system.[31]

Quotas can contribute to global justice

A Contraction and Convergence framework of global quotas has the potential to contribute hugely to global justice. The recent "make poverty history" movement has demonstrated a moral awakening and a will among the affluent to see justice created world-wide.[32] But with this as with so many other things, individuals cannot create different systems. Global quotas can create new systems and new forms of wealth and ensure that wealth is evenly pre-distributed to all citizens of the globe. The trading of quotas brings money to poor countries as a right, not as aid.

By insisting on equity, Convergence addresses the objections of "less developed" economies to paying for the damage caused by the "developed" affluent countries. Poor and vulnerable countries and communities are most at risk from the climate change that results from global warming, even though they are the least responsible for causing the problem. And those who are already cash-poor have fewer immediate resources for escaping from or coping with the effects of climate change. Trading in quotas is a way to create a world of greater social justice. Exactly the same arguments apply for individuals: everyone plays by the same rules; we can be flexible within the broad regulations; we can if we wish go below our personal target and then sell quotas and benefit financially. Ultimately, carbon-thrifty citizens or countries know they are not subsidizing their more carbon-profligate neighbors.

International quotas harness all countries in the effort to halt global warming. As the imperative to cap emissions becomes clearer, the most important question is how to draw all countries of the world into the Contraction process. If everybody is to participate, it is crucial that we apply a principle of fair rules and benefits for all through trading. Global quotas allow countries – like individuals – to reach their goals in a variety of ways. They also provide encouragement to continue to make cuts way beyond any agreed targets, since that will mean they have more carbon permits to sell, or fewer to buy.[33]

Complementary interventions

To make Contraction and Convergence work smoothly and have the best chance of being accepted, governments would need to make it as easy as possible for people to make the changes that it will require. Reducing carbon emissions by 90 per cent is going to mean some radical changes, especially in transport and home heating (in colder countries). It is essential that other, complementary, top-down interventions take place to help people cope with these changes. All of us can act "green" and make individual changes, but only up to a certain point: there are many things we simply cannot do for ourselves.

Public transport

The market advantage will lie with public transport, when the reduction of carbon emissions makes private car use very expensive. But in many countries, services will need to be hugely improved. First, they will need to be made as carbon-efficient as possible by using renewable electricity to power buses, trams and trains. Second, systems will need to offer a frequent, reliable, comfortable and accessible service. Public transport must become attractive and available to all. And the more people who use public transport regularly, the safer and more pleasant it will become. Third, complete services must be put in place all at once, not in a phased-in way, so that people can give up their cars and still easily get to work, education or social engagements. Improvement in services must not take the form of a piecemeal response to dwindling car use.

Help for those living in sub-standard housing

Other kinds of regulations would also have to come into effect. For instance, with regard to housing, buyers and tenants would be severely disadvantaged if they had to buy or rent homes that were not properly insulated and ventilated; their carbon quotas would not go as far as those of people who could control the way their homes are built. So the regulations governing housing standards would have to be uniformly high, and would have to be rigorously enforced. While upgrades were taking place, governments could create legislation whereby developers or landlords purchase extra quotas to give to residents in the winter if the accommodation supplied was sub-standard.[34]

Support for eco-production

Various forms of eco-production would have to be actively supported and encouraged, and the link between energy and carbon broken as much as possible by developing renewable sources of energy. International agreements would have to eliminate all subsidies to polluting industries and those subsidies that create low prices for fossil fuels and energy derived from them. Every business or industry – any kind of enterprise – would have to meet strict criteria for ecological soundness. Also, the precautionary principle would have to apply: if there was any doubt about ecological safety, a project could not go ahead.

Can Contraction and Convergence actually happen?

Some people tell me I am naïve to promote such a radical measure, especially individual quotas, and to suggest it could happen at an international level. When I outline the framework to groups, they often accept the necessity of capping, even see the fairness of apportioning equally the entitlements to emit; but they say that, politically, it can never happen. Others say that if Contraction and Convergence were really as good as I claim, it would have been adopted by now.

The radical nature of Contraction and Convergence does act against it to some extent. Strong regulation is unpopular in free-market growth economics, because it limits people's freedom to behave more or less as they will, in the pursuit of profit without taking the common good into account. Nevertheless, if banks can be brought under state control, which has happened in several cases recently, and if governments can consider international cooperation when they perceive a threat to the world economic order, the same can happen for carbon emissions if the political will is there. Regulation under a Contraction and Convergence framework is much less intrusive than the kind of regulation where people are constantly monitored in terms of carbon emissions. It encourages markets and trading that are open to all; it is fairer than the current EU Emissions Trading Scheme, and it has more certain outcomes than taxation.

Nevertheless, the idea of the global commons, which is central to the framework, challenges the ways hyper capitalism has allowed small numbers of commercial interests to appropriate and profit from something that belongs to all of us. We cannot pretend that giving everyone their fair entitlement to the atmosphere is not radical and is not going to change global commerce. But the framework is not anti-market, anti-money, anti-profit or anti-trade. On the contrary, it sees them as essential elements of vibrant, moral and ecological economic activity, with maximum participation and benefit for the greatest possible numbers of people.

One of the functions of both national and international government is to make the world safe for us. Global warming constitutes a genuine threat to our safety, greater than banks going to the wall and ultimately greater than international terrorism.[35] Curbing global warming is a social goal that concerns all of us, and towards which everyone needs to work. But members of the public, concerned though we may be, cannot participate fully if the public processes to do so are not in place. Constructing such processes is a job for governments. We need to persuade people in a position to make the rules to regulate us for our own good, to establish the limits of action, but to guarantee the maximum of freedom within those limits.[36]

Governments fear that they will not be re-elected if they are the first to introduce policies that rely on a concept like quotas and the regulation they imply. But if they could engage in a little long-term thinking, and if political parties could work together, they could probably convince the electorate that carbon quotas would be the ultimate give-away budget: everyone would profit both in the long and short term. It would be an attractive way to cooperate and harness a spirit of emergency for the crisis facing us.

Citizens and non-governmental organizations (NGOs) can lobby governments in order to convince them to regulate, and to do so using the best possible processes. (See the section below on Cap and Share, for an example of NGO activity.) We also need massive publicity and education programs, which deal equally with the need for capping and the principle of fairness in any process for capping. The education process is simultaneous and two-way; governments and people have to take the initiative at the same time, and they also have to educate one another. It is essential to create a climate of opinion where political parties that support Contraction and Convergence will not fear being penalized.

Some people object that the necessary world-wide regulation is not possible. International inter-governmental work is needed, in order to push for world-wide adoption of the Contraction and Convergence framework. The EU could take the lead in this, having already begun to address the need for carbon-reduction, even though the Emissions Trading Scheme (ETS) is currently poorly designed. And global organizations such as the World Trade Organization (WTO) could have a huge role to play. This is a way to make globalization more democratic and beneficial to all.[37]

We have the global organizations and the communications capacity for worldwide regulation. It is too early at the time of writing to know what kind of global governance may emerge from the recent financial crisis, although increasing numbers of people are calling for rules, principles and regulation. But air-traffic control is one example of such global cooperation. We also brought in worldwide regulation of the chlorofluorocarbons (CFCs) that were destroying the ozone layer. During the 1980s, legislation was introduced which succeeded in curbing them so that the hole in the ozone layer did not get any bigger. We have the advanced computer technology that would be required for issuing, tracking and trading carbon rations. We would need a global programme of registering all citizens so that they could be issued their quotas. The vision and the will to put the principles of capping and sharing carbon emissions into practice are what count most.

This book is all about possibility, about humans' capacity to fulfill their ecological and moral potential. We must explore and advocate sound routes ahead, even if they currently seem politically impossible.[38] Public concern about global warming is growing, and that could affect greatly what is politically possible. The unanticipated or the "seismic" event often does occur, and it is important to be intellectually and emotionally prepared when a political opportunity suddenly arises.[39]

The Cap and Share campaign: first steps

Cap and Share is the name of a campaign launched in late 2006 to lobby governments to start a Contraction and Convergence type process in Ireland and the United Kingdom, and also to persuade their EU partners to do so. Cap and Share proposes a number of steps, beginning with transport then extending to the whole of the EU Emissions Trading Scheme. The campaign also has a good proposal for reserving some quotas for the first twenty years in order to assist regions that have particular climate-based difficulties in adapting to reduced carbon emissions. The idea is that the Contraction and Convergence framework could eventually be globally accepted, following the EU lead. The campaign needs the concerted efforts of ordinary people; why not you?[40]

The science of global warming is compelling more and more politicians to take it seriously in spite of commercial and political difficulties. Any country or union of countries such as the EU could put a Contraction and Convergence-type process in place immediately. A country or union that leads the way will show moral and practical leadership by example. It will also facilitate the development of that region's ecologically sound technical innovations, which will give it a market advantage.[41] You can be part of this movement quite easily. Having read this chapter, you have the basic ideas, which are being refined all the time in a wiki (an online development of ideas in which all can participate) on the Cap and Share website.[42] You can also get information there about lobbying and spreading the word.

Conclusion

This chapter has been about finding the fairest form of regulation in the drive to contain global warming, so that we can have the freedom to live decent-quality lives on a healthy planet. In the chapter, I have emphasized security, fairness and equity as important underlying principles for developing methods to reduce carbon emissions. I have also introduced the notion of the global commons. We will meet all of these themes again in the next chapter, which discusses how a Citizens' Income can assist a reduction in demand in the world economy, thus helping to control global warming and contributing to sustainable development.

CHAPTER 5

FINANCIAL SECURITY

If a society is serious about living sustainably, then it must guarantee every citizen basic needs as of right.[1]

In this chapter, I consider another radical proposal that is morally and ecologically sound, namely a Citizens' Income (sometimes also called universal benefit or basic income guarantee). Under a formal Citizens' Income scheme, each citizen would receive a regular and unconditional cash income from the state. Everybody, whether they did paid work or not, would receive this and they could spend it as they pleased. This would replace social welfare benefits as we currently know them, and, most importantly, it would also extend to people who are not currently in receipt of state benefits. Ideally, a Citizens' Income would be sufficient for each person to live a simple but satisfying lifestyle without supplementary income from paid work.

This radical proposal has huge implications for social justice, in that it provides security for all in ways that means-tested social welfare and a minimum wage cannot do. Security is a prerequisite for reducing economic demands to sustainable levels, and for creating a social and cultural climate where everybody is free to act on their moral and ecological concerns.

A Citizens' Income receives almost no attention in the mainstream media, probably because it challenges so many of our taken-for-granted ideas about work, money and quality of life. I address these issues later in the chapter, but for now it is worth knowing that Green parties in all countries promote the idea, as do some organizations of the unemployed, NGOs promoting economics for sustainability, along with a number of Christian groups. In Ireland, for example, the Conference of

Religious in Ireland (CORI) is strongly in favor, and was at the forefront of the drive for the government White Paper in 2002.[2] Governments in Austria, Finland, Brazil, Argentina, Japan and Quebec have also shown interest in the principles behind a Citizens' Income policy.[3]

Financial security for all

A Citizens' Income ensures that everyone has basic financial security, without adding to pressure for economic growth as a source of income. Currently, the only way most of us can get money is by exchanging our life energy for it, in a job or other form of paid work, with welfare as a fallback if we become unemployed. Some people don't have to work to get money; they inherit wealth, or get money from investment, gambling or other sources. Others, through saving, frugal living and financial intelligence, have created a situation for themselves where they can cut back on paid work.

The current global economic system produces conditions where people have to struggle every day to compete and survive. Some are struggling for material survival, whether in poor countries, or in pockets of poverty in rich countries. It can be difficult to think morally and ecologically when one is preoccupied with basic survival from day to day.

The struggle for survival also applies, though in a very different way, to those affluent people in the minority rich world who are coping with busy lives of commuting, job, earning, spending and keeping up debt repayments. Many of us are wage slaves who cannot see a way to get off the treadmill of work, because we have to earn money to service a mortgage and/or other debts, or because we feel we have to maintain a certain lifestyle. The system also forces businesses and people to compete with other businesses and individuals, in order to survive.

Struggles for survival often result in denial or emotional

numbing; we push away feelings of unease or even of deep concern about the state of our personal health, and the health of the world at large, because we must service our debt. Lack of time can also lead people to buy the most convenient goods and services, which are not usually best for the environment or for social justice.

Sometimes a lack of cash forces people to buy the cheapest food, even if it is also of the poorest nutritional value, or if it means that farmers are squeezed by supermarkets to keep shelf-costs down, and in turn have to resort to bad farming practices. They can afford only the cheapest clothes, even though the clothes have been made by sweatshop labor. (Nor is this to ignore the fact that many expensive designer clothes are also made in sweatshops.)

Linking security, reduced demand, and reduced growth

Poverty, stress and a competitive environment do not always prevent people from being concerned with moral or ecological issues. Many people on very small incomes are careful to spend ethically, buying local and fairly traded goods whenever possible. But in general, the more we work, the more we buy. The poorer we are, the harder we find it to afford ethically produced goods. This cycle drives growth.[4] The growth system thrives when people participate in a round of working, earning, spending and servicing debt. We are encouraged very early in our lives to take on debt, so that we are always going to have to do paid work to service that debt. We are also encouraged to spend money on getting concentrated relief for our ills: joining a gym, having massage, acupuncture or other treatments, taking short breaks and eating convenience foods. Drugs, including coffee and alcohol, also provide short-term relief. Our need for money ties us through our work to the large corporations, whether or not we work directly for the corporations (many of them are now contracting out more and more functions and concentrating on product development and marketing).

But it is in nobody's long-term interests to continue with untrammeled economic growth (see also Chapter 2). If we give financial security to everybody, as of right, the need to work at our current high-speed rates is lessened. Consumption then decreases, since with less intense work-lives, our need to spend is also lessened. Reducing consumption is essential for developing steady-state economies that do not destroy the earth and its inhabitants.[5]

A Citizens' Income benefits both the poor and the affluent. It gives those on welfare a way out of the poverty trap: if they get decent paid work, they don't lose benefits, as they do on means-tested welfare. It gives mortgage-slaves and harassed workers a chance to step back from the work-earn-spend treadmill: their Citizens' Income provides enough for the basics. A Citizens' Income also gives workers increased bargaining power within their jobs because they are not reliant on income from work to supply basic needs.

Given a level of basic financial security, people can develop all sorts of economically dynamic and intelligent carbon-neutral activities, because they have psychological space and actual time to be creative. We don't remove paid work altogether, we just lessen its ability to drive growth. Virtuous systems would have a chance to develop in place of the vicious cycles we have now. It is hard – even impossible – to predict the exact nature of these virtuous systems, because of the dynamic nature of any system, and the impossibility of knowing how different elements will interact within a system.

A Citizens' Income will, however, have two effects that we can be reasonably certain of: it will change the nature of work so that people have more time to act on their principles and their concerns about ecology and morality. It will also lessen demand for consumable goods, thus reducing demand on the earth's resources.

Equity: a prerequisite for security

Security, if the term is to be used with any credibility, must be equally available to all. One part of the world or its population cannot consider itself secure if other parts are under pressure for survival. Socialism tries to reform capitalist economics and create equal security for all. Essentially, socialism relies on the redistribution (by means of taxation) throughout the entire population of wealth created in some sections of the population. This redistribution was often achieved in questionable ways in socialist states. In addition, socialism sees no problem with creating wealth by means of economic growth (see Chapter 1).

A Citizens' Income creates security by pre-distributing wealth and, in doing so, it tackles the problem of growth. As later parts of this chapter make clear, it is a way to reform the capitalist system, towards the classical vision of a free communist society. No country supposedly practicing communism has truly aimed for the vision of Karl Marx, as described in the quote below. With a Citizens' Income, the means for achieving this reform of capitalism are radically different from those proposed by the traditional critics of capitalism.[6]

> ... in classical Marxism, socialism is just an instrument for achieving the society in which people can work freely according to their abilities but still get enough according to their needs. If we now see a number of problems with socialism – threats to freedom, problems of dynamic efficiency, etc – then why not harness capitalism to achieve the very same objectives? Why not go for a capitalist road to communism?[7]

Socialism has been largely abandoned by nation states and the radical alternative of a Citizens' Income is yet to be put in place. Many countries now attempt to provide a safety net for citizens by means of two mechanisms: the minimum wage and the provision of unemployment and other benefits. But both of these ultimately go against morally acceptable and ecologically sound economics. Neither mechanism provides the level of security required for sustainability.

Problems with a minimum wage

A minimum-wage arrangement requires growth, no matter what the cost. The minimum wage is based on two assumptions, one compatible with sustainability, one incompatible. The first assumption is that everyone is entitled to an income sufficient to live on. The second – problematic – assumption is that this income should come solely from paid work. But a minimum job-wage at a level that trade unions would regard as satisfactory would actually make it difficult if not impossible for many – especially small – employers to meet wage costs. [8] This gives rise to at least two further problems.

First, employers are tempted to cut costs outside of the wage arena. For example, large supermarkets force down prices to farmers,[9] which has a spin-off effect on farming practices.[10] Businesses may lay off one set of workers and take their work to cheaper workforces, or to places where they can cut costs because environmental regulations are lax. Thus, even if a minimum wage is in place in one's home country, one's job may not be secure.

Second, society at large (governments, people and trades unions) becomes concerned with creating new jobs and maintaining existing ones, regardless of their ecological or social effects. As long as a living income is tied to jobs, then jobs will have to be created, regardless of the consequences, environmental or otherwise.[11] Ultimately, a minimum wage results in the kind of untrammeled growth that destroys security.

Problems with welfare

Welfare systems, although they are often referred to as social security, actually reduce security. Most welfare schemes are means-tested: if claimants take up employment, they start to lose other vital financial benefits such as rent allowance and medical card. They also pay income tax and social security contributions. But the net income from the job can often leave the claimant with much less overall than when welfare payment, rent allowance and medical expenses were combined. This situation is usually referred to as the poverty trap. Currently, the trend is to reduce welfare rates, in order to make people do paid work. Once again, the concern of society becomes the creation of jobs, no matter what kind, so that people do not claim welfare. This puts a premium on economic growth and it leaves people little choice about entering the poverty trap.

With a Citizens' Income, citizens would still receive the basic income if they took a job and this would be a way around the poverty trap. Currently, those who take paid work without declaring it, while also claiming benefit (which they are not supposed to do), are acting very sensibly, when one examines their situation closely. They are avoiding an outrageously high real rate of taxation. Means-tested benefits impose very high actual rates of taxation on those who receive them.[12]

Most of the better-off are aware of the poverty trap, but it does not affect them, so few are motivated to do anything about it.[13] Moreover, since those on welfare are often seen as a burden on the rest of society and since people sometimes make fraudulent claims for welfare, means-testing is widely seen as a way to control claimants. But if any society is serious about creating an ecologically and morally sound economy, it must provide basic necessities to all of its members. If it denies the basics and insecurity becomes endemic, then growth will become the only means by which people can survive.[14]

But a Citizens' Income also has huge benefits for those not claiming welfare. It is for every single citizen and this would allow many to step off the work-earn-consume treadmill by cutting back on the time spent in paid work. It would also give a basic income to those who currently receive no state or other payment, but who participate in caring work or other forms of work that are not financially rewarded.

The simplicity of a Citizens' Income also gives it an advantage over means-tested welfare systems. These systems are very complicated to administer, making them time-consuming and costly. Tax credits and special exceptions for helping people to avoid the poverty trap are in place in many countries. Yet all these special rules make it extremely difficult for people (staff and claimants alike) to understand the schemes. The more complicated a scheme, the more likely it is that mistakes will be made and the more difficult it is to computerize it.[15]

To ensure fairness, administrators have to ask for a lot of detail about claimants' lives and circumstances. This means that those who are entitled to benefits sometimes do not claim them because the process is intrusive. With a Citizens' Income, there is no doubt about eligibility. As with carbon quotas, a Citizens' Income scheme has everybody playing by the same rules in a simpler system. Everybody receives it, by virtue of being a citizen; it is not a handout to those seen as less fortunate or for those considered a burden. The straightforward administration would also involve a big saving in costs.[16]

Paying for a Citizens' Income

Taxation
Several thinkers on Citizens' Income have imagined only the income-taxation route to paying for it. It is true that many affluent countries could currently finance a Citizens' Income scheme quite easily with taxation revenue. In this scenario, capitalism, having developed the productive potential of the rich countries to a degree unimaginable a century ago, would now be perceived as having laid the foundation for a new balance

between work and other life activities, by financing Citizens' Incomes.[17]

One could argue, however, that such a system would erode its own tax base. But unless an economy has been so abused that it cannot even produce enough to provide basic necessities for its citizens, there will always be enough wealth circulating or economic activity whose proceeds can be shared for this purpose.[18]

Persuading taxpayers of the value of financing a Citizens' Income from income tax could be difficult. Under a Citizens' Income paid for by taxation, the tax burden would be shifted onto the shoulders of those higher up the income scale. At the same time, they would get the benefit of a guaranteed income not linked to work. Unfortunately, few better-off people currently see this potential benefit to themselves. Most concentrate only on the fact that a Citizens' Income would also support those who pay less tax. Since the better off are more numerous and generally get more attention from government than the less well off, their votes are valuable and governments do not want to alienate them.[19]

But how could taxation pay for Citizens' Income in countries where many live at a subsistence level and do not pay tax? Some wealthy individuals can pay tax but money could also come from the international sphere, in the profits of mega-corporations and financial markets; in the cancellation of poor countries' debts; in closing down tax havens and making corporate taxes mandatory.[20] The New Economics Foundation (NEF) conservatively estimates that global fossil fuel subsidies, paid to rich corporations out of the public purse, amount to $235 billion annually. Just one year's worth of these subsidies could wipe out all of sub-Saharan debt and start financing Citizens' Incomes.[21]

Aid donations from rich countries could also be diverted to Citizens' Incomes. One of the problems with aid as currently organized is that it goes to governments and not directly to citizens.

It is also possible to impose taxes on international currency exchanges. There have been some signs that world leaders can think in encouraging terms. For instance, at Davos in January 2005, Jacques Chirac (then President of France) called for increased taxes on international financial transactions in order to finance a war against AIDS. If it can be done for AIDS, it can be done for a Citizens' Income, once leaders understand the benefits.

So there are potential sources of finance for Citizens' Incomes in countries without large income-tax revenue. Some who have identified such sources of money advocate using it for "kick starting" economies in poor countries.[22] But kick-starting usually means stimulating unregulated growth, which is highly undesirable in the present circumstances. It would be far better to use the money to finance a Citizens' Income, which gives people that little bit of cash that allows them to move away from complete reliance on subsistence farming.

At the same time, we need transnational organizations such as the World Trade Organization (WTO) to shift their focus and work towards global agreement and legislation to ensure that all economic activity is ecologically sound.[23] The conditions that a Citizens' Income would create, in combination with legislation for ecology, would probably result in the eventual decline of the large global corporations and the rise of localization. But before the global corporations began to decline, their profits could be used very effectively. And as the next section outlines, there are other sources for financing a Citizens' Income, namely natural earth resources.

Earth resources

Taxation (on income and on the subsidies and corporate activities mentioned in the previous section) is not the only possibility for financing Citizens' Incomes. We have seen in Chapter 4 that capping and sharing carbon rations on a global scale could provide a type of Citizens' Income, through trading of quotas. But that source would decline as the surplus became less and less; our carbon quotas would get smaller with time, and so less trading would be possible. However, the notion of getting income from this source is linked to the idea that all of us, as citizens of the planet, have a right to the commons, the earth resources that belong to everyone.

As examples of the benefit to citizens of earth resources, in Alaska each resident receives about $1,000 dollars per year as a dividend on state oil resources. In Norway, almost oil revenue goes into a public pension fund. As another possibility, if airwave licenses were being issued, government could sell them to TV or radio companies, instead of giving them free of charge, as they do now. Currently, companies can make profits for their share-holders from something received for nothing, but which belongs to all of us.

Those who own land could pay land dues to the public finances, and all of us would receive a share of it. For those who own very little land the share we receive would be much greater than the share we pay. Those who own no land would pay nothing, but would receive their dividend nonetheless.

Many countries, such as Denmark and Australia, already have some form of value tax. Hong Kong – that bastion of free-market capitalism – has no private land ownership at all. Land is owned by the state and leased. A land value tax is hard to avoid. The world's super rich who spend much of the year in London but avoid paying income tax could not avoid the tax on a big house in Mayfair.

This is a not a new idea. Adam Smith argued two centuries ago that such a tax was a "peculiarly suitable" way to raise revenue since it did not distort people's incentives to work, save and invest. Churchill favored a land value tax, as did Lloyd George.[24]

Land tax is based on the idea that the revenue that comes from using the global commons, which belongs to all of us, should be issued directly to citizens. The principle is that every single citizen of the globe is entitled to a share in the earth.[25]

One could argue that nobody has any right to dividends from the earth. But we currently have a situation where some people benefit greatly, and others not at all. In such circumstances, it would seem better to say that everyone has equal rights, which should be equally apportioned.

Politically, there is a lot to be said for taking the source for a Citizens' Income away from taxes on earned income. This would be very popular with the middle-earning classes, who pay the most tax, in most systems. Their taxes pay for most welfare provision, with little apparent benefit to themselves. We have already seen that the universal entitlement to a Citizens' Income would be attractive to people in this very group, who rarely if ever have to rely on welfare, but who would all be entitled to a Citizens' Income. They could even offset it against tax if they did not want to use it for daily life.

Using earth resources to finance a Citizens' Income also connects economics and ecosystems. Getting dividends from the earth's resources might make us feel a stronger or a renewed connection to it, appreciate it more and become better protectors of our provider.[26]

How much?

A Citizens' Income should allow any citizen anywhere on the globe to live a decent frugal life, without having to top up the income with paid work. It should be possible to work out how much is sufficient for this in any given country. Philippe Van Parijs, one of the foremost thinkers on the subject, suggests that in the short term we are thinking of a basic income that would correspond to roughly half the current guaranteed minimum income for a single person.[27]

Old political differences will not disappear. For example, debates will continue about whether families or individuals should get allowances. Some will also believe that a Citizens' Income should be high, with everyone responsible for their own health, education, housing, transport, waste disposal, and other services.[28] Others will believe that it should be lower, with most services free or at a nominal cost. The main thing will be to keep the focus on the beauty of sufficiency and a philosophy of *enough*, rather than creating pressures for exponential economic growth. Richness would reside in the security of knowing one always had enough. Insecurity and anxiety are debilitating. For most people, a richer life would be one free from financial insecurity and fear of poverty.[29]

Even if it were initially introduced at levels lower than an income sufficient for all the basics of life, a Citizens' Income would be worthwhile, as it would still provide a way out of the poverty trap. If it were introduced at a very modest level, those who became unemployed could still receive an extra benefit while out of work, and would continue to receive their Citizens' Income if they took paid work. It would also allow harassed workers to cut back to, say, a four-day work-week, thus giving themselves some relief from the treadmill.

Who gets it?

Many will assert that those who do not do any kind of work should not receive payment from the state.[30] In fact, we already have a situation where people get money without work: from inheritance, investment, gifts, rents, capital gains and gambling. The real problem in the minds of some is with the poor: why should they get money "for nothing"? Equally, most people do not acknowledge that there is a huge background of social and community resources behind everyone who has money or the capacity to earn money. Everybody receives gifts from the community in all sorts of forms, but the distribution of those gifts is unfair.[31] A Citizens' Income apportions those gifts more equitably and provides more people with the chance for empowerment and individual choice. And this policy does not give citizens huge sums of money, just enough for a decent livable level of welfare, provided we manage the money well. If we want more, we can choose to work for it.

Maybe to start with, though, there could be some kind of participation requirement. A participation income would cover everyone involved in a wide range of activities that contribute to society, including, but not limited to, paid work. Examples are household work, parenting, care work, retirement, educational pursuits and all the activities that currently fall under the heading of voluntary work. Very few people do not want to participate at all in society, and eventually it would probably not be worth the administrative trouble of refusing a Citizens' Income to people like that, so that in the long run, everyone could receive it.[32] It could certainly be introduced immediately with regard to pensions, by introducing a certainty of state pension at a good livable level.[33]

Currently, jobs are seen as one of the chief mechanisms for creating social inclusion.[34] Jobs involve people in the labor market and give them spending power so that they can consume on an equal footing with others. But the emphasis on inclusion through jobs devalues and disadvantages other activities that create vibrant and inclusive communities, such as voluntary work and unpaid caring work or low-paid creative or political work. A Citizens' Income will give people more freedom to participate in this kind of work. In this way, it will also give participatory democracy more space to grow and will allow people to be involved in developing solutions to our current ecological and social problems. (See Chapter 8 on citizen-leadership.)

In fact, there will always be some inequality of outcome under a Citizens' Income scheme; not everyone will want to work for extra money, and the income on its own would provide for a simple, sustainable lifestyle, not for luxuries. Nor is a Citizens' Income a magic wand; to live on it, people would need to manage their money well. Many of us would have to re-educate ourselves financially.

Who qualifies as a citizen?[35]

The question of who is a citizen is currently a thorny one, given large-scale global migration. But the question of how long somebody needs to live in a state before being considered a citizen or eligible for welfare is not new.[36] For a start, however, if global Convergence and carbon quotas (see Chapter 4) were implemented, travel would be more expensive and people would migrate less. But at the same time, the income from trading in carbon quotas could make conditions in one's home country more pleasant. Global quotas will also enhance conditions for local economic activity. It may also be possible to pay for a Citizens' Income in the home country from other sources as outlined earlier in this chapter. The incentives for economic migration will then lessen.

There is also something to be said for giving immigrants, even if they are not citizens, a basic income on a par with the Citizens' Income. This demonstrates a model of equity and security in the host state, and could have the advantage of spreading knowledge of a Citizens' Income to immigrants' countries of origin.

Environmental stability and a sense of global sharing, promoted by international legislation including global carbon quotas as proposed under the Contraction and Convergence framework, would also contribute to peace in currently war-torn countries. War and hostile relations between states contribute hugely to environmental degradation, poverty and consequent migration.[37] With peace and security improved in every country, eventually all people could live decent lives in their home countries. We would migrate mostly for adventure, love, cultural exchange and education.

Every citizen would need to be registered in their home country (they would also need to be registered to receive their carbon quotas under Contraction and Convergence). Currently, millions of those who survive outside the growth economy do not officially exist. People who are trafficked and enslaved for various purposes are largely untraceable. Registration would not be easy, given the circumstances that make millions of people practically invisible to officialdom. But registration would have to be a goal.

As already mentioned in Chapter 4, registration has other benefits: while people remain unregistered, they do not officially exist, and they cannot make the smallest transactions that all of us take for granted in "developed" countries, such as getting a loan, or owning property.[38]

Like Contraction and Convergence, a Citizens' Income *does* require a form of pro-active governance, and some people object to that, or say that it is not possible. But the kind of governance in question is very different from that of a "nanny state". While people have to be registered, they are not required to account for their every action, nor are they monitored in detail. These proposals provide security where it counts (in income and in energy and with regard to global warming) and allow citizens of the globe to make creative decisions, differing according to time and place, in other aspects of their lives.

We also have to take into account that the notion of citizenship has expanded in recent times. It refers not just to citizenship of a state, but of a bio-region and of the whole globe. Ideally, world politics would eventually be organized so that people could receive earth dividends based on the resources of their bio-region, rather than their nation-state. A bio-region is a territory defined by a combination of biological, social and geographic criteria, rather than geopolitical considerations; it is a system of related, interconnected ecosystems.[39] This would mean that if a region had been divided politically, so that one state had most of the natural resources, residents of other states in the region would not suffer.

How work could be transformed when decoupled from money

A Citizen's Income challenges the notion that the only way one is entitled to money is to do paid work. It decouples work and money to some extent but does not break the link between them completely. Work can still be a source of money, but not the only one.

Unfortunately, if we have to depend on paid work for survival, then many of us have little choice about the *kind* of work we do. We have to ignore or repress the social, moral and ecological consequences of much of the work that takes place in the name of economic growth. The spiritual exhortation to align our work with our values is laudable, but impossible for many.

Work, as many know it now, has severe personal, familial and social consequences. Work organizations often require their employees to prioritize the organization. Such organizations need to be reshaped and if this does not come from the top, it could come from the bottom, provided workers have a secure income that is not tied to their jobs. It would allow them freedom to shape their relationship with their employing organizations. Greater numbers could participate in paid work, but reduce the time spent at it.[40]

Work is one of the chief ways we relate to the world. A Citizens' Income would free us from our dependence on exploitative or morally dubious paid work and allow everyone the chance to do rewarding work, in relationships, self-development, family, creative pursuits, and other intrinsically rewarding activities.[41] It would allow us to enact principles and values in a range of situations apart from our jobs. It would also allow us to do creative, political and social work, which contributes hugely to society. Such work is usually badly paid, but with a Citizens' Income one could do it and still have a decent income. A citizen could participate in education, at any time, with the backing of a Citizens' Income. If people wanted to work on the land or spend time growing more of their own food in their gardens or allotments they could easily try to do so. If a person did earn so much that the Citizens' Income was not necessary to live well, she or he could donate it to a good cause.[42]

Weakening the link between work and money is hugely significant. It is a liberating experience in that it allows one to disengage from work that is personally alienating or harmful to the earth or to other people. A number of good programs already show how individuals can weaken this link by living simply and developing financial intelligence.[43] With a Citizens' Income this chance to be discerning about the kind and amount of work one does is available to everyone, not just those lucky enough to inherit wealth, or to have developed their financial intelligence, in a culture that plays down the possibilities for such development. The opportunity to be discerning regarding work constitutes genuine choice, as different as could be from choices currently available, such as what brand to buy or how many TV channels to have.

A Citizens' Income could also reinvigorate traditional public-service jobs, which include education, health care, transport, defense, policing, librarianship and postal work and the provision of utilities like electricity, water and waste disposal. People used to take up work like this because it provided a possibility to enact principles and values of serving one's community. But public service is sometimes not very "efficient", dealing as it does with people and their complex needs. So enacting one's principles is becoming increasingly difficult as cost-benefit efficiencies and value-for-money pressures permeate more and more public-service workplaces.[44] But the transformation in bargaining power for workers, which a Citizens' Income would provide, could have the effect of transforming public-service workplaces also.

In recent times too a great deal of low-intensity and apparently low-skilled work (although often high in people skills) has also been lost: work like park-keeping, play leading and bus-conducting. Such work is very important in maintaining a friendly and authoritative presence in public places; it keeps streets, parks and public transport safe and attractive.[45] But it has been eroded in the drive for "efficiency" and the need to pay minimum wages. A Citizens' Income could make such work more attractive, because low pay would not mean a low overall income.

Running a business would also be a different kind of experience. The income from it would be a top-up to a Citizens' Income. People would be free to try out business ideas, and the businesses would be viable as long as they made some small profit. They might even be able to carry losses for a short time while the business got established. As long as the business was ecologically sound there would be every chance to try out entrepreneurial ideas, and there would be no harm done if the business failed, because the people involved would have their Citizens' Incomes to fall back on.[46]

It is difficult in the present climate for businesses to act ethically, when they have to remain competitive on an international market. In recent times, many have tried valiantly to make the business case for fair trade, going organic, or ethical investment, for example. But the hard-headed business case for these is not always convincing: fair trade is not always as profitable as so-called free trade. A Citizens' Income could reduce costs to employers and make it easier for truly ethical businesses to survive.

Socialists may object to these new possibilities for business as "subsidizing employers". But the employee is in a much stronger position with a Citizens' Income than without one. Employed workers would have greater bargaining power and would always be in a position to strike or resign if working conditions were poor. They would have a financial cushion, separate from their jobs, to tide them over a period without wages.

A Citizens' Income would also allow businesses to run a natural life cycle, fulfill a purpose and then die off naturally. Businesses that are successful often reach all their potential customers, serve them well, and then go out of business because their market has been saturated.[47] They have cycles, like everything else in nature. However, in modern growth economies, a business is not regarded as successful unless it is constantly expanding and we find it hard to accept as natural that businesses come to an end. Businesses reaching the end of natural cycles are seen as failing and, instead of preparing for it, the business leaders allow them to die horrible deaths.[48] They often leave behind unemployed workers and bankrupt creditors. Or else society hysterically tries to prevent the demise of particularly prominent corporations, often by using taxpayers' money to prop up these dinosaurs, which only postpones the day of reckoning.[49] Responsible employers may try to keep a business going, in order to maintain employment. But in doing so, they are often forced to take the business in a direction that does not fit with ecological and moral principles.

A Citizens' Income would allow us to work with the natural cycles of business. All workers, from the entrepreneurs to the employees within a business, would have the security of their Citizens' Income to fall back on when a business reached its natural end. And given the vibrant economic activity we could expect in the long term under such new arrangements, new businesses would regularly emerge to replace old ones.

A Citizens' Income would also allow for the enforced closing of businesses that are socially or ecologically harmful, such as weapons producers or big polluters.

Trade unionists generally do not like these ideas. The notable exceptions are in unions with high female membership or low-paid workers. They have realized that a Citizens' Income would enhance the market for part-time and unskilled labor. But the unions are in general wedded to the idea that money should come only from work, and they are concerned with people as workers, not primarily as citizens.[50] A Citizens' Income is based on the idea of money as an entitlement that accompanies citizenship – of a state and of the planet. On the whole, though, the principles behind a Citizens' Income are entirely compatible with unions' core concerns about workers' wellbeing.

A Citizens' Income scheme ensures security in the basics, but allows initiative (and / or competition) for anything else, provided enterprises are sufficiently eco-friendly. This leaves the way open for all kinds of private enterprise for those who want it, but means that those who do not want it are still secure in their basic needs. Thus, both sides of the old left-right divide get most of what they want.[51] We get buoyant economic activity, within a context of reduced demand and reduced growth; any growth will have to pay its way fully; and all citizens, including those in paid work, have financial security and greatly increased individual choices.

Harassed workers on the work-earn-spend treadmill are also generally in favor, when they learn about a Citizens' Income, but they are not usually formally organized. There is, however, great scope for a time movement (if only people had the time to get involved) and a Citizens' Income could be one of its objectives.

Conclusion

In this chapter, I have outlined only the most basic of the principles and effects of a Citizens' Income. Apart from mentioning a land tax, I have not discussed the serious issues of housing and accommodation, which will be a crucial follow-up to the introduction of a Citizens' Income.[52] The notes to this chapter provide a direction for further reading, and I have also listed additional resources.[53] I have concentrated here on two foundational issues regarding a Citizens' Income. First, there are the principles of social justice and ecological soundness which underpin it. Second, there is the way that financial security for all reduces economic demand, in turn easing pressures on the earth and its people.

A sense of *enough* is one of the cultural factors that could create a climate where people might be receptive to introducing a Citizens' Income. Even while we wait in hope that governments will put such a system in place, we can all start to develop this sense of *enough*, with regard to our personal finances. It is worth investigating now the books and programs designed to help us develop financial intelligence and live well on less money.[54] This can help us to escape the work-earn-spend treadmill and live well on modest incomes, whether our country's economy is booming or in recession, within the current economic system. In this way, we benefit personally but we also benefit the environment when we consume less. And should a Citizens' Income be introduced eventually, we will be very adept at living well on a modest amount of money.

The principles informing a Citizens' Income help us to ask radically new questions about the nature of both work and security; such questions are radically different from those dominating the hyper-capitalist world. The next chapter turns to food and we shall see that a Citizens' Income would also be a positive factor in helping to support Intelligent Agriculture and create food security for the world.

CHAPTER 6

FUTURE FOOD

Let us imagine a world of plentiful high-quality food and good nutrition. Imagine millions of local agricultural systems, expressly designed to feed people, delivering reliable and sustainable food yields in harmony with nature; farms and gardens of an appropriate scale and a contribution to environmental stability. Alongside, we would have humane conditions for animals, prosperity for farmers and a balanced ratio of farmers to non-farmers. Worldwide, many more people than at present would live on the land and be involved in working it and caring for it. This would encourage thriving local communities and reshape the ways we understand living in the countryside.

Applying principles of *enough* – following sound ecological and moral codes – in agriculture can get us to this state.

If we had an agriculture of *enough* worldwide, we would no longer have the situation we have now in affluent countries, where many are obese but undernourished at the same time; they have more than enough quantity, but not enough nutrition in their food. In other parts of the world, those currently existing on a poverty diet would have food security and good nutrition, combined with excellent local cuisine.

The idea is often put forward that the world cannot feed itself from traditional agricultural practices, and, therefore, needs industrialized agriculture. This restricted view of the future of food comes from a lack of historical awareness. Every country in the world is capable of feeding itself with healthy produce from its own traditional agricultural practices, provided its farming systems have not been disrupted.[1] Disaster and famine have occurred when traditional systems of agriculture have been destroyed by colonial interference. The present-day equivalent of such interference is known as "structural adjustments", whereby countries receive aid or international loans, but on condition that they adopt certain economic policies, such as growing cash crops for export. War, dictatorship and invasion have also disrupted traditional systems, as do more recent global warming and associated climate change, storms, flooding and drought.

Intelligent Agriculture

An agriculture of *enough* is intelligent because it responds to local soil and climate conditions. It has also been called craft-level farming, ecological farming, local farming, and enlightened agriculture.[2] It does not matter what we call it; I have chosen to use the term "intelligent" for the most part, because it is so different from the suicidal industrial agriculture that dominates farming policy today and which many of us take so much for granted that it is commonly called "conventional" agriculture.

Intelligent Agriculture is currently taking place in pockets all over the world.[3] It takes its cues from ordinary farmers and cooks and the craft and knowledge about food and farming that they have build up over centuries. It draws on and conserves the collective skills of entire societies, but it is not stuck in the past, because it builds on those skills in ways that suit changing local climates and environmental conditions.[4] It draws on a principle of harmony with nature in its dynamism and responsiveness. So it pushes forward craft knowledge, and it draws on the best of modern science to do so. Permaculture, for example, is a fairly recent development that mimics natural forest systems. It can cope with severe weather conditions and can even reclaim land in desert areas, which conventional farming treats as uncultivatable.[5]

Intelligent Agriculture gives us healthy and flavorsome diets, with a great deal of variety, mostly based on plant food, but supplemented with a little meat. Its variety gives us the best chance of getting all the nutrients we need. The diet is not exclusively vegetarian, because small amounts of free-range meat are good for human health. Raising animals and fowl, on an appropriate scale and with a right philosophy, is compatible with ecological principles and good for the soil.[6] Low-intensity cattle-rearing is carried out in landscapes that contain grass, hedges and copses, which can absorb carbon-dioxide from the atmosphere, thus mitigating global warming. Again, it is a question of finding the right methods and appropriate numbers.

Intelligent Agriculture gives preference to arable farming, favoring staple crops in the places where the different ones grow best. Then it fits in horticulture and pastoral farming or animal husbandry around and alongside them. In this way, it works a huge variety of livestock and crops, organized in complex systems, which can take advantage of every detail of local landscapes and weather conditions.[7] This results in maximum variety in a farm, making it robust in the face of potential pests and diseases and resilient in the face of global warming. The diversity of crops and the intensive attention of the farmer mean that crops are not blanket-sprayed with pesticides. Small numbers of animals per farm, integrated with all a farm's other activities, mean much less methane than in large-scale operations. The result is manure that can be easily managed and used as an essential conditioner to maintain soil fertility.

In intelligent agricultural systems, the task of food production is with the masses of ordinary people.[8] This is in direct contrast to the present trend for a few producers to mass-produce food. Maximum participation does not mean that everyone has to be a farmer (although we need many more farmers than we have now); it means involvement in a food culture, even if not growing food. It also means many people involved in allied trades and crafts such as baking, butchering, cheese-making, brewing and wine-making. And although not everyone has to be a farmer in the sense of making one's primary living from farming, it does broaden the definition of farmer to include gardeners and those growing only a small proportion of their food. Gardening is therefore a part of Intelligent Agriculture. It is extremely productive if judged on the yield per acreage.[9] A huge amount of food can be grown on balconies and in small gardens, especially if vertical spaces are used to cultivate climbing plants.

Food from Intelligent Agriculture is organic in the best sense of the word. While many organic farmers currently farm following principles of Intelligent Agriculture, many more are industrializing their operations. This industrialized organic farming often sticks to the letter rather than the spirit of the organic movement. The result of Intelligent Agriculture is beyond any narrow labels that are open to abuse, and is truly ecological. Pests are controlled by biological predators, companion planting and biodiversity. The skill and knowledge of the farmer or grower ensure the health of the plants, animals and soil. The well being of the land and animals comes about as a matter of course, because they are within a healthy system. It takes knowledge and a high degree of skill to do this kind of farming.

Intelligent Agriculture also operates on a principle of making a good living for farmers and agricultural workers because not only are the land, soil and animals important, people are too. It is possible to generate adequate income for many from agriculture, while still keeping an ecological and moral code. There is a role for profit in accumulating capital for further investment or development, but this is very different from the generation of maximum cash returns for small numbers of shareholders, which drives the industrialized system

Intelligent farmers avoid expanding their operations for the sake of growth; they do not strive for uniformity of produce, but make a virtue of seasonality and local variety; they do not invest in advertising to reach far-flung markets, but rely on reputation and word of mouth. And they avoid fossil-fuel energy as much as possible and use renewable energy. The resulting food supply chains are short, simple and direct, ensuring freshness, safety and animal welfare. If a food chain is truly local, then buyers are likely to have a relationship with the farmers and to be aware of the practices involved, how animals are treated, and how pesticide is used. Short supply chains encourage knowledge, whereas long chains encourage ignorance and allow us to turn away from the conditions of food production.

Intelligent Agriculture is not export-focused because no country can have food security if it relies heavily on trade for its food. The principle here is to first meet local food needs, so that countries and bio-regions become self-reliant. The myth that affluent countries do not need to grow food is seen for the folly it is. There is room for some global trade in foods that can travel well without depending on flying, but customers pay a financial price that reflects the true cost of their production and trans-portation. There is also room for food aid from surpluses, since the principle of subsistence at home is in fact the best guarantee of givable or marketable surpluses.[10] Of course, the more that Intelligent Agriculture is practiced worldwide, the more each region can become self-reliant in food; the need for food aid would gradually wither away.

Already, in Ethiopia, for example, the agriculture ministry is working to restore the traditional mixed farming that can keep the country from dependence on food aid. It has a policy of self-reliance in food and is turning away from coffee as a cash crop. Food aid is in any case in jeopardy under the industrialized system of agriculture. Countries like the US are facing lower yields due to drought, high oil prices and land going out of food production to grow crops for bio-fuels.

Cuba is also an example of how a potentially poor country avoided dependence on aid or loans and the conditions attached to them. It did this not through government planning, but through the initiative of ordinary citizens. During the soviet era,

Cuba was an ally of the USSR and the USA prevented Cuba from importing oil and fertilizers. People started growing food in even the tiniest urban spaces. There are now 8,000 community gardens and urban farms in Havana alone and 50-80 per cent of the food supply is cultivated and provided from within the city limits. Beef farmers also raised cattle on sugar cane, when the USA stopped importing Cuban sugar. Thus, Cuba has for many years been self-reliant in food, giving it an independence that many poor countries do not have. The country grows enough food for its entire population, so that it does not need to trade if trade is not to its advantage. This is the basis for fair trading, and the power to trade fairly is a result of Intelligent Agriculture in all cases.[11] A country can trade when it will gain something from the trade, but can refrain from doing so if trading will disadvantage it.

Balancing urban and rural

With Intelligent Agriculture as the norm, farming becomes the occupation of many more people than at present and it also becomes the biggest employer. This rebalances the relation of urban dwellers to rural dwellers. Rebalancing in affluent countries is a restoration of people to the land. In Britain and the USA, for example, it would mean a change from the present 1 per cent of people on the land, to about 20 per cent. In countries where 90 per cent or so currently work the land, such as Uganda, Rwanda, or Ethiopia, it would mean getting 50 per cent of the population off the land into trades and professions so that there are enough electricians, plumbers, builders, doctors, teachers, engineers, lawyers and so on. Intelligent Agriculture therefore goes hand in hand with planning the non-farming work in any economy. But the remaining 50 per cent have to be encouraged to remain on the land and they have a market in the 50 per cent who do not work the land.

As part of the rebalancing, farming has to be promoted for the worthwhile and intellectually challenging occupation that it is. Rebalancing challenges the modern trend where small numbers work the land in industrialized agriculture, and most others commute to office or service jobs, or leave the land altogether for such work. Rebalancing also helps prevent the growth of sprawling suburbs or shanty towns around cities.

Social life

In the past, the traditional mixed farm worked well ecologically and was a vital part of thriving local economies. But that kind of farming was often accompanied by family and social relationships that were less than ideal. Societies built around Intelligent Agriculture value tradition in terms of farming practices, but they question the personal oppression and social isolation that so often went with the old ways of life. Intelligent Agriculture takes for granted a spirit of equality and respect among those who work the land, because it is important that humans flourish, as well as soil and animals. It operates on a principle of thriving rural communities where there are plenty of local social activities as well as work. Modern communications also facilitate contact with others from all over the world.

To support these thriving rural communities, we would also need dispersed healthcare and education. The trend for industrialization and centralization in agriculture is mirrored in hospitals, schools and universities; those disciplines need to follow an ecological model also (although that is more than I can go into in this book).

Farming in a good social environment and a supportive household network (whether with a blood family or a chosen one) is a good way of life. Intelligent farming is healthy hard work, which is also skilled and interesting, and at the same time, one has a very satisfying connection with nature and the seasons. Farming and allied crafts such as butchering, baking, cheese-making and so on are valued as an essential public service. Young people are encouraged to go into farming and food trades because such work is intrinsically rewarding and challenging and because it makes an essential contribution to society. The work available contrasts with the alienating work of industrialized farming, or the rather meaningless work of many services and in information technology. While the work is hard, it contrasts favorably with what is available to most urban and suburban people or commuters today: they work very long hours, but without the connections with nature and the land afforded by agricultural work. Good agricultural work is also far better than unemployment or the black-market labor such as begging or prostitution, to which some people are forced to resort when they leave the land.

In short, Intelligent Agriculture results in a restoration and valuing of agrarian societies across the world, with a parallel recognition of the high skill involved in agriculture, and high status for craft-level farmers everywhere. But this kind of agrarianism is not about going back to the past. It is built on a modern understanding of universal human rights to dignity and fairness. It makes full use of electronic communication, which is another gift from modernity. The new agrarianism is also postmodern and postindustrial in a very sophisticated way. As the basis for an economy it requires a high degree of knowledge and creativity, arising out of a culture that values ecological and social harmony in equal measure with technology.

Getting there: reform of the Common Agricultural Policy as a model for western countries

In modern societies, where most people are divorced from the sources of their food, we need wherever possible to set up formal policies that reward people for involvement in any form of agriculture. If our policymakers accepted the principles of Intelligent Agriculture and the importance of food, they could put them into practice with reform of agriculture policies, as the

Ethiopian government is doing. As an example of a European model for doing this, Christopher Lloyd has made suggestions for reforming the Common Agricultural Policy (CAP) of the EU in ways that are much more radical than those currently suggested by EU decision-makers.[12] (For more on CAP, including the reforms already in place, see Chapter 3.) This model for reform could be put into place in other affluent countries also.

Most decision-makers in EU agriculture recognize that there is a need to reform the CAP at this time. But there is a need to put in place much more radical reforms than those currently suggested. The CAP – or any state's agricultural policy – could be treated as a way forward for a total re-visioning of food production and distribution. Incentives should be provided to everyone who grows their own fruit and vegetables, and they should all be classified as farmers.[13]

The precise details would have to be worked out, but, to start, there are a number of broad principles. Anybody who grows their own food qualifies for a subsidy and therefore benefits financially. To qualify for a subsidy, one must adhere to agreed standards set for organic production. Any products sold through retail outlets that are not produced within, say, fifty miles of the point of sale will be subject to a surcharge. Thus, consumers who insist on buying non-local produce will pay a premium. Food that travels a long way is thus disadvantaged in the market place. This encourages local production and consumption while helping to reduce carbon emissions on food transport. The surcharge on non-local food will become a source of finance for the country's agricultural policy, supporting publicity, education, research and administration.

The issue of subsidies may not appeal to all, but they are certainly a way to quickly get more people involved in food production and to promote a public conversation about food and agriculture. Greater involvement in food production always has huge social and environmental benefits. People eat more healthily, we think more about what we eat and learn where it comes from; we are more sensitive to nature and to our environment, we get more exercise, along with a sense of fulfillment from eating food we have grown ourselves. And local markets for food can thrive.[14]

Local authorities would have to make more and more allotments available in order to facilitate food growing for those who do not own land and to avoid discrimination against those who do not have access to land. Ideally, all house and apartment designs would facilitate growing of some kind and planning regulations could be changed to include that requirement.

What about the poor countries that are currently being encouraged to develop cash crops in industrialized settings and to export food? If citizens in affluent countries consume more and more local food then the world trade in agricultural products will decline. This will have repercussions for those "developing" countries that have been encouraged to join the world food market as it currently exists. Ideally, reforms in agricultural policies would be accompanied by reform of the World Trade Organization (WTO), which currently encourages a global food market with free trade and competition. It would have to support the principle that food should be consumed locally and transportation of food minimized. If it were playing a role in Contraction and Convergence (see Chapter 4), this would complement such work on food. But the principles of agrarianism and Intelligent Agriculture differ in every respect from the principles on which the WTO, the World Bank, the EU and the UN are currently working globally. Their policies dovetail also with those of large corporations and most governments.

Policy reforms such as I have outlined would be a great way to encourage those who are already engaged in Intelligent Agriculture. They would also get more people involved, and, worldwide, create food security. But it is not likely that the necessary worldwide agricultural-policy or WTO reforms will take the shape outlined above. Nevertheless, as in the case of Contraction and Convergence and a Citizen's income (see Chapters Four and Five) it is important to think big and to envisage the schemes that national governments and global organizations could put in place and support. Sometimes, an extraordinary event does happen, which makes government do a turnaround and look for truly radical policies. Then, it is important to have sound frameworks to offer as alternatives.

Creating Intelligent Agriculture outside formal structures: a worldwide food movement

The most likely scenario for building food security is that in most countries ordinary people will have to take the lead and make it happen. In Cuba, ordinary people, not government, initiated the resurgence in agriculture. Government there is now stepping in and making more land available for agriculture, but it is taking a lead from citizens. So the rest of this chapter is about starting from the other end and having citizens lead the process. Worldwide, many are doing so already and this could be extended into a recognized grassroots food movement. The food movement would create a food-growing and -supply chain based on Intelligent Agriculture, parallel to the industrial food system. Government may eventually be educated by the citizens and introduce policies to support a new food and farming culture.

The food movement is about all citizens' rights to food security, to enjoy sound nutritious food of the highest quality, and about farmers' rights to be respected as people who work the earth for the benefit of all. The movement recognizes food as having huge environmental, cultural, nutritional and local economic value. Moreover, this movement is already happening; we just have to make it stronger and get more and more people on board. The huge numbers of good food and agriculture projects that are already happening – farmers' markets, allotments, courses in gardening and growing, Slow Food – are all part of the food movement. It includes any kind of agricultural endeavors where industrialization has not taken hold and it is also a massive educational project. The affluent may drive the food movement financially at the start, but there is every possibility to bring poorer people on board. It will have benefits for all, including the less well off, in the long run. The industrial food system benefits nobody, either in the long or short terms. And it doubly disadvantages the poor. (See Chapter 3 for more on the industrial food system.)

A food culture

The food movement is also about the thought-shifts we need to engage in and the values we need to acquire, in order to create a food culture. In a food culture we all want to seek out good food, produced locally. People also recognize the satisfaction and the pleasures of cooking and eating together, since a true food culture includes these rituals and relationships.

Food is a keystone in personal health and well-being, and in the resurgence of Intelligent Agriculture. Thinking differently about food can get us to an intelligent state in agriculture. Because we all eat every day, the possibility exists to increase interest in food quality and food security and to connect people's interest with the sources of food. In this way, everyone can acquire some understanding of farming, instead of distancing ourselves from the source of our nourishment. Such understanding restores an appreciation of the earth's bounty and how it provides for us even if we are not directly farming it. Good cooking, sound nutrition, enjoyment of food and Intelligent Agriculture go hand in hand. This essence of a food culture is what already drives the Slow Food Movement.[15]

A food culture is not the same as the modern definition of having lots of expensive restaurants, while cooking and eating at home are downgraded. Restaurants are important, but alone do not form a food culture. Nevertheless, chefs have a big role to play in extolling the virtues of super-fresh local and seasonal food. They can also put the spotlight on farmers and food preparers who supply them and can help those producers get more custom.

No knowledge could be more important than how to grow and prepare good food. Universal cookery classes in schools would be a great boost for the food movement. Career guidance could also make information available regarding food-related occupations such as butchering, cheese-making, baking, making preserves and so on. It could value them as interesting and absorbing work and promote them on an equal footing with currently more popular occupations such as information technology and tourism. But until our education system formally includes such issues in its curriculum, parents, teachers, adult educators and other citizen-leaders can show awareness of such occupations as real possibilities, and talk to learners young and old about them. The trades involved could get together for an educational and promotional campaign detailing how the work is varied from day to day, how it demands intelligence and skill, and is of value to society. In a food culture, this would be common knowledge.

Getting rid of the obsession with cheap food

A crucial step in creating a food culture is to get rid of our current obsession with cheap food. Industrialized farming and eating have become acceptable and have escaped scrutiny because such large numbers of the public have been convinced that food should be cheap on the shelf. Cheap industrial food suits the project of untrammeled economic growth. If food prices can be kept down, then people will spend their excess money on other consumer disposables and contribute to "growing the economy". We have bought the myth that if food is cheap, society benefits because consumers have cash to spare. But we are confusing social benefit with an increase in GDP.

Many people in affluent countries are horrified by the thought of having to spend more, as oil shortages and global warming make food more expensive to produce, even under industrialized conditions. In a food culture, we would be prepared to spend a greater proportion of our disposable income on food. In the US, the average is 10 per cent; in the 1950s, it was 20 per cent. In Europe, the average outgoing on food in 1970 was 32 per cent of income; in 2007 it was 15 per cent. At the same time, great numbers spend 12 per cent on mobile-phone charges.[16] Most people could spend more on food if they chose to. It really is a matter of prioritizing how we spend our money. If we want to support local farmers and let the industrial system fade away, we have to get the money to where it matters.

It is essential to recognize that there is no such thing as cheap food from the industrial system. Industrialized food is costly in terms of carbon and methane emissions and in terms of human and animal misery and soil degradation. It also is subsidized in many cases. But none of these is factored into the shelf price. You get what you pay for and with low shelf prices we also get water pollution, antibiotic resistance, food-borne illnesses and countless other dangers to the environment. These are costs to society and we *do* pay for them out of the public purse. But because they are hidden, food from industrialized agriculture seems cheap.

Given a straight and obvious choice at a poll, most people would vote against all those downsides of industrial agriculture. We need to make the "unstraight" or less obvious choices too. Eating in modern times brings together the personal and the political like no other human activity. We need to actively choose to lose our ignorance: the industrialized system depends on us looking the other way, or being kept in the dark and satisfied to be kept there. Cheapness and ignorance go hand in hand. Giving up our ignorance can be hard to do because it is a philosophical choice that is about resisting a powerful system.

At this stage, the argument is always made that the poor need cheap food, even if it is industrial. For a start, this is implying that the poor do not deserve better quality. But this argument also ignores the fact that the cheapest and healthiest food is cooked from scratch using good basic ingredients. You can be healthy and eat affordably at the same time if you know how to cook and avoid ready-prepared supermarket food. The modern food business has developed in such a way that kitchen skills and know-how have been lost to many, especially to the "bottom" layers of society, and official policies do nothing to change this. To lack the skills of cooking and growing is a form of poverty. It is political activism to restore foundational skills of growing and cooking and to share them with other people, so that reliance on the industrial system, including supermarkets, dwindles. Work like this empowers people, restores health, and is ecologically and morally sound. Some local authorities are also supporting classes that teach young people, especially parents, how to cook using fresh food and this is to be applauded and encouraged.[17]

Formal structures to support the food movement

A social movement such as a food movement can be extremely dispersed, with many non-formal initiatives. But it also benefits from formal organizations to promote it. Colin Tudge has suggested structures to support a worldwide food movement. First, he suggests a worldwide food club, which would bring together all the good initiatives – formal and informal – that already exist, in a more organized way, not to make them uniform, but to make them available to each other and to avoid duplication. He also suggests a college for enlightened agriculture, which would develop practical, scientific and philo-sophical knowledge about food and farming.[18]

The worldwide food club

The worldwide food club is a cooperative of concerned customers, quality producers and food preparers. It is truly a cooperative, based on a pact, whereby the producers undertake to adhere to standards of Intelligent Agriculture, the preparers prepare to the highest standards and customers undertake to buy from them no matter what. It is also a club because all these people are members, who decide what the standards should be, for production and for belonging to the club. The notion of club is important, because clubs have the potential to be democratic. The members elect their leaders, but they also have the power to get rid of them if they abuse their positions or do not run the club according to agreed standards. The worldwide food club is not exclusive; anybody can be a member, as long as they are committed to the food movement, its dedication to high-quality food, food security for every world region, and the ecological and moral principles that underpin such aims.

The grand task of the food club is to match the food culture with the suppliers and to ensure that the transactions are fair to all concerned. No other organization has precisely this aim, although many other organizations are compatible with the worldwide food club. For example, the Slow Food movement is dedicated to creating and supporting a food culture. Compassion in World Farming is concerned with the treatment of animals. The Fair Trade movement seeks equitable trade.

The functions of the club are co-ordination and organization. To begin with, it would concentrate on developing a global exchange of information via a website. It will make it possible for farmers, preparers and consumers to connect with each other, thus developing relationship farming and marketing.[19] It will allow new suppliers to get access to a local market for their food and it can also direct customers to existing schemes. The market is central to the worldwide food club because it is the most vital connection between eaters and producers. But it is a politicized market, completely different from "consumer pressure" on the existing market.[20]

The only meaningful guarantee of quality in one's food is when one knows who produced and prepared it. Markets that arise out of this desire for quality could thus be referred to as relationship markets.[21] Relationships are formed when farmers can sell high-quality produce as directly as possible to the customer. They can do this by using farm shops and farmers' markets, as well as local butchers and truly local grocery stores. Cheese-makers, bakers, jam-makers and other food preparers who know the farmers would also be important elements in such marketing. Relationship marketing means money as directly as possible into the pockets of the farmers and small producers, without most of it being sliced off by supermarkets. It allows critical connections to develop, which then foster the circulation of all kinds of information and knowledge about food and farming.

Buying-clubs can also be part of relationship marketing. They can serve people in cities who cannot buy directly from farm shops or farmers' markets. A group of city dwellers can, for example, put in an order to a farm with the farmer delivering to just one house, which acts as a clearing site for the rest of the buying-club members. Expenses for the farmer are minimized by having to deliver to only one location.

The club never encourages intelligent farmers and food producers to participate in or compete with the industrial model of agriculture. It avoids the industrial model's emphasis on productivity and the production of ever-more "units" at an ever-lower price. Intelligent agricultural enterprises have to operate in a separate sphere where even small producers can make a profit. It is about creating a new food chain, parallel to the old one, and in the hope that the old one will eventually wither away. The market for good food needs to stay completely outside the industrial markets, which includes supermarkets and large food processors.[22]

All this circulation of information would initially happen through the website, which would itself have to be set up and maintained. Volunteers would probably do it at the start but there would also be a need for paid staff. The club must remain non-profit, and trustees would be needed to ensure that its work always adheres to its founding principles.

Eventually, the club could acquire a physical presence. Shops or marketplaces would allow people to shop in person for food they might otherwise buy online through the club's website and links. The shops and markets could also sell food from further afield, as long as it was produced according to principles of Intelligent Agriculture, and was traded fairly and voluntarily. The trust could also aim to buy land for the food club. This would allow more people to get into farming, either as low-rent tenants of the trust or as farm managers.

The successful operation of the worldwide food club depends on humans drawing on their capacities for cooperation, trust, and care. It takes an optimistic view of human nature, as different as can be from the idea of the never-satisfied, acquisitive and ruthlessly competitive sovereign consumer who supposedly drives the industrial economy. This whole project of a food movement is about transferring power over food to the masses of ordinary people worldwide, who value the wealth in good food and food security.

Sympathetic organizations would also be listed on the website. For example, Slow Food, Compassion in World Farming, the International Society for Ecology and Culture (ISEC), The Foundation for the Economics of Sustainability (Feasta), the New Economics Foundation (NEF), time movements, Citizen's Income groups, along with campaigns for access to land and redistribution of land ownership. One goal of the movement is to include all sections of the community, poor as well as affluent. The worldwide food club could probably advance this goal through working with sympathetic organizations and activists that are already trusted by poorer people. Any government could choose to support the food movement by supporting and funding the worldwide food club, provided it did not impose conditions on the club's activities.

The college for enlightened agriculture

A college is a collection of people who have the same aims, a bit like a club, but with an emphasis on education and research. Its main strands would be a think-tank, a practical-skills section, a scientific research section and a teaching and learning section. It would bring together, in a virtual community, farmers, scholars, researchers and teachers from all over the world in the many disciplines relevant to Intelligent Agriculture. One of these disciplines is gastronomy, which in its most ecological form goes way beyond recipes and how to prepare food. Gastronomy links agriculture, animal husbandry, sociology, anthropology and political economy.[23] There is already a university of gastronomy in Italy, which has two physical campuses.[24] It was founded in 2003 by the Slow Food Movement in co-operation with two regional authorities.

The college of enlightened agriculture would examine practical questions of food and agricultural skills and create a bank of knowledge concerning traditional farming skills, as well as more recently developed systems such as permaculture and agroforestry. It would develop knowledge about natural pest control and enhanced methods for maintaining soil fertility without recourse to oil-based fertilizers. It would research the most humane and ecological ways to rear animals and to use animals for labor on farms.

The college would study the issue of self-reliance in food for each country, or at least for each bio-region. It would research the best ways to reform food policy in different countries and trading blocks such as the EU. The industrial-farming lobby is strong at national and global governmental level and the college of enlightened agriculture could provide biological and economic research to support groups lobbying for intelligent agricultural policies.

Related to this, the college could also study the development of a fair global trading system for foods that certain countries cannot produce. Bananas, chocolate, oranges and spices come to mind as luxury goods for those of us living in temperate climates. But it would probably be necessary for countries within a bio-region to engage in some trade of non-luxury goods also. This would not be against the principles of Intelligent Agriculture, since self-reliance is different from complete self-sufficiency. Fair and ecologically sound trade would be judged on how fair a price was paid for the crop and how the crop was grown. Growing it must not prevent people from growing food for their own needs. The means of transport must also be carbon-neutral.

The college would also examine the growing of crops for bio-fuels and how these might be fitted into small mixed farms in appropriate quantities, but without jeopardizing food supplies. It would consider issues of genetic modification and where that might be used as a force for genuine good, distinct from the immoral practice of patenting seeds or creating terminator seeds (see Chapter 3).

Researchers would also investigate further how no-dig or no-plough arable methods of cultivation can contribute to soil fertility. In such systems, green manures and winter cover crops mean that soil is never bare, and the continually growing plants are always photosynthesizing and thus removing carbon dioxide from the atmosphere. In contrast, plowing lets oxygen come in contact again with the soil, where it reacts with the carbon to form carbon dioxide, which is in turn released into the atmosphere. No-dig or no-plough methods prevent this. They also use far less machinery and hence less carbon-emitting fossil fuels, unlike the fossil-fuel dependence of current industrialized agriculture. Soil can also renew itself with properly managed grazing.

These methods also mean the land absorbs 30 per cent more carbon dioxide from the atmosphere than "conventionally farmed" land and can thus play a part in mitigating global warming.[25] Plants take in carbon dioxide as they grow, the carbon turns into plant matter, and some of it is lodged in the soil. The oxygen is released back into the air. Researchers and farmers are also developing perennial grains and vegetables, which require no digging at all. Some of these developments may take time, but they can work if there are no pressures for high yields.

Research in recent times has concentrated on selecting crops that maximize yields under irrigation and chemical fertilizers (which make money for their manufacturers). A great deal of money is spent on pesticide research because that is profitable. Very little is spent, however, on researching biological methods of pest control that would make pesticides unnecessary.[26] The college could emphasize research on varieties that perform well under the kind of soil fertility that would increase in intelligent agricultural systems. It could also investigate how good science can help Intelligent Agriculture to engage in precision-farming. For example, scientists could determine exactly when and in what amounts to apply nitrogen fertilizers so that there is maximum take-up by plants, and no run-off of excess fertilizer into water courses. Further studies could examine how to continue to strengthen natural systems, to include studies into how farming can support a rich and varied wildlife in every country.

The college would also examine questions about the best ratio of rural to urban people, how to encourage people to take up farming and how to support them, how to distribute educational and health services evenly between rural and urban areas and how to make farming incomes equal to those in non-farming jobs.

Culture, attitudes and values would also be a concern, as well as the development of economic and political theory concerned with supporting a core principle of *enough* in agriculture, and indeed in all human endeavors. The college would work with all of those researchers who already are well disposed towards this worldview, and would support a huge teaching and learning project to promote it. This would include work on an appropriate 21st century worldview for science and the scientific community. Many scientists already support the principle of working in harmony with nature and this kind of work needs to come to prominence. Science also needs to restore an ethic of public service in order to promote human, animal and soil well-being. We need to work out how to value and reward good scientists who look at the big picture and work for the planet as a whole, rather than purely for profit.

Traditionally, people's knowledge of land and nature developed slowly over time. It is still the case that such deep knowledge cannot be hurried, but at the same time there is a certain urgency about building up resilient food systems. The college would need to develop ways to transfer the knowledge that already exists to future generations, along with passing on the mass of new knowledge that is constantly emerging about intelligent systems.

Is food security really possible?
Of all the proposals I have surveyed, Intelligent Agriculture is the most possible. It forms the basis of an alternative, parallel knowledge economy, for something that really matters: food. It is the movement that is most in the hands of ordinary people and that is not dependent on government, national or global. Government policy supportive of Intelligent Agriculture would be great, but we cannot rely on elected politicians to put it in

place. In any case, individual governments would not have the global reach of a mass social movement. A food movement can create a parallel food system outside of the industrialized structures. A culture can "pop" ecologically; it can take off and flourish in ways unforeseen, when the right elements are in place and favorable connections are established among them.[27] As with all questions based on *enough*, we are talking about creating a new kind of future. We have the possibility of enrichment if we respect good traditions and, at the same time, work on new ways of organizing, thinking and acting.

CHAPTER 7

POLICY AND PRINCIPLES

The last three chapters introduced three policy proposals: Contraction and Convergence, a Citizens' Income and radical reform of agricultural policy. Chapter 6 also looked at a food movement, a less "official" but equally possible change for agriculture and food. Each proposal embodies principles of security, equity and care, and each one has the potential for exciting, imaginative and quite dramatic change, which is also ecologically and morally sound. The proposals are living, adaptive and dynamic because they encourage creativity and diversity for groups and individuals around the world. Behind each proposal lies the desire to foster deep democracy and justice. Taken together, they would strengthen each other and have even greater potential.

The implementation of Contraction and Convergence and / or a Citizens' Income would be the icing on the cake for Intelligent Agriculture, because they would create conditions to favor all locally produced goods, including food. The job-free time that people could choose if they had a Citizens' Income would also allow greater involvement in growing and preparing their own food. A Citizens' Income would help struggling farmers to stay on their land and work it for the benefit of all in society. It would also allow people to work as employees in agriculture without fear of exploitation. Thus, the agricultural skills in society at large could grow. Contraction and Convergence, which would have a huge effect on transport, would give local growers an advantage in the marketplace.

Like *enough*, the attitude at the heart of each of them, the proposals' full potential cannot be accurately predicted from where we stand today, although imagination can help us to see their possibilities. They are not, however, about a return to some golden era of simple local and rural pleasures. Simplicity, locality and the rural feature strongly, but given the global reach of the problems, the solutions need global dimensions. Ideally, the whole world, every nation and state, would be involved, because ecological insights show us that everything is connected. This means that countries cannot go it alone: one cannot be truly secure if its neighbor is not secure.

The bossy-boots in me wants to simply impose Contraction and Convergence, a Citizens' Income and Intelligent Agriculture on the world immediately. Unfortunately, or maybe fortunately, I cannot. Perhaps it is fortunate, because many people in the minority affluent world (the Euro-Atlantic English-speaking sphere) would hate them and consider them to be regressive or invasive and would react badly. On the other hand, if the proposals were put in place, those same people might be pleasantly surprised at how much the quality of life would improve. In turn, this would give them breathing space to see the world differently and to eventually welcome the philosophy of *enough*, which underpins the proposals. Most people want to do good, but significant social and economic barriers stand in their way, as things are currently organized. The proposals would remove many of these barriers.

There is every chance that the proposals would be welcomed in the majority world because there they could create conditions for many kinds of vibrant economic activity. But this economic activity would be different from what the minority affluent world has taken as the norm for development: economic growth that creates financial riches for small elites, while disadvantaging ordinary people and degrading natural systems.

The vision of unregulated growth "works", in the sense that it brings short-term material wealth to small groups in the countries where it is practiced. But it also affects our understanding of the term "development". Development comes to mean increasing levels of consumption. It implies that the ideal state for all is to live some version of a suburban lifestyle, commuting to work, with salaries, pensions, cars, and various other possessions seen as essential to modern life, along with speedy foreign travel. This ideal state is supposedly available to anybody who complies with the work-earn-spend system and is willing to be productive and to compete with others. We are required to use our creativity and imagination in the service of profit and for "growing" our economies in this narrow sense. But our imaginations have been constrained by this worldview, to the extent that we have largely lost any understanding that progress and advancement for the human race can take many other forms. Throughout the minority world, there is a reluctance to ask hard questions about the nature of progress; as a collective, we are not willing to question a system that is causing our problems.

Within a worldview of *enough*, it would be more appropriate to say that *all* societies (the so-called underdeveloped as well as the "developed") require transformation. In other words, all societies on earth today need a fundamental shift in values and worldview: they need to converge around the idea of deep security. And this security has to be based on equity and justice. It is not simply "security of the fittest" while the weak die off.

The modernist worldview that underpins the affluent minority way of life has given us many good things, including ideas about justice and human rights. These can serve us well; the Contraction and Convergence framework, for example, is modernist in its assertion that everyone has equal rights to the global commons. Nevertheless, we need to recognize that a modernist worldview has considerable downsides. The biggest of these is that modernist culture sees the world as just another resource, which provides raw materials that humans can use. These raw materials have no life of their own and we have no relationship with them beyond exploitation. As a result of this outlook, we have lost a sense of ourselves as ecological beings, embedded in and dependant on natural systems and connected to every living thing on earth.

Another modern impulse is to look at individual parts and assume that if we fix each one separately, then all parts will work well together. This might work well for a machine, but the world is not a machine, even though modernist thought often conceives of it in this way. This is where the notion of "kick-starting" economies comes from, because this is what one does with engines or other machinery. The current global economic growth system creates vicious circles, which governments and international lawmakers try to control and manage with piecemeal initiatives, or attention to minutiae. But it is impossible to undo vicious circles by tackling individual parts of a system. This is like tackling only the symptoms of an illness and not its deeper causes.

Governments that put in place any one of the proposals will be international leaders in tackling causes, ensuring security in a just way. They will put in place a deep stability, in food, income and environment. This core stability, existing at the broad parameters of our systems, can foster maximum diversity within those parameters. It is not the same as being static: in healthy ecological systems, there is constant change, growth and renewal of a cyclical kind. Nor is stability the same as control. Deep security and stability are dynamic and self-organizing once they exist in a whole-system way, and they are not possible through the current system. People who are very attached to the modern worldview often denigrate human desire for deep security and stability, painting them as boring and restrictive and putting too many limits on human initiative and the capacity to take risks. In fact, those who do propose *enough* in hypermodern societies take big risks, because we are often dismissed as crazy or unrealistic.

In all economic activities, whether they contribute to growth or not, two principles stemming from *enough* need to apply: sustainability (that is, respect for ecological systems and staying within biological limits so that the systems we depend on can continue) and security for all (which is also a form of social justice). Sustainability is too often taken to mean sustaining hypercapitalism by finding ways to continue unregulated economic growth. Security is too often equated with controlling unruly elements and defending borders.

True sustainability and deep security are absent from our current economic policies. In fact, current economic policy makes people feel insecure, so they feel the need to take any kind of work, no matter the social, environmental or human cost. It is very difficult for people who are insecure in their income and livelihood to do things from day to day that lay the foundations for future sustainability and justice.

Keystone attitudes

Healthy ecological systems always have keystone species. Biologists take the idea of the keystone from architecture, where the keystone is the tapered stone at the top of an arch. Without it, the whole arch would collapse. In the natural world, certain species function as keystones in their ecosystems. For instance, alligators in the Florida Everglades create "gator holes" that fill up with water and provide a habitat for a diversity of smaller creatures. If the alligators disappear, then all those smaller creatures also die out.[1] Green cover crops are keystone species for soil health, and soil in turn sustains all food production. We need keystone policies that are underpinned by a vision of a rich social, personal and economic habitat for people. The role of politics is to design institutions, regulations and policies that enable people to co-operate, that ensure democratic accountability and that facilitate citizens to act for the good of the whole community and the whole earth. The policies outlined function in this way. If key principles are observed or key attitudes

143

developed, many structural problems can work themselves out in practice.[2]

Contraction and Convergence, Intelligent Agriculture and a Citizen's Income may not be the only frameworks capable of providing stability and security. Even if those particular frameworks are rejected, the principles behind them – stability, equity, and an emphasis on the whole system – should be the primary goal of all governments, lawmakers and citizens. To summarize the keystone attitudes:

- Deep stability, rather than control, is the overall attitude.
- Equity, sharing and a fair apportioning of resources are core principles.
- Unlimited creativity, innovation and imagination are encouraged within the broadly defined parameters that provide security and stability.
- Both local and global dimensions of collective security and stability are always a central concern.
- Whole-system performance is what counts.[3] The emphasis is on creating virtuous circles where every inhabitant gets the nourishment it needs, from a rich collective environment.
- Systems are designed for resilience. That is, they are designed so that they are capable of persisting in the face of human error, acts of aggression or so-called "acts of God" such as drought, floods, storms or earthquakes. If one part of a system is destroyed, the other parts are not so badly affected that they cannot keep going.
- The goal is to provide the richest possible choices to maximum numbers of people, as distinct from unlimited choices for small numbers of people and poor quality choices for most.
- Systems are democratic in the sense of being structured to facilitate meaningful participation by maximum numbers of people. Great things are possible when we increase

participation.[4]

- Simplicity is a core aim. Policies are easy to understand, administration is straightforward and the system is thus protected from fraud. But simplicity is not to be confused with being simplistic or simple-minded.

Policy based on good principles can also show people what is possible, so that we can tell ourselves new stories about human potential. It activates imagination and a sense of possibility. Good policy can revive people's sense of themselves as ecological and moral beings, connected to others in a healthy system. Many eco-villages and communities currently – and very diversely – represent some of what is possible.[5] The challenge is to bring such possibility to all people of the earth.

The choice to live by such keystone attitudes is a moral one. It is also political in the broadest sense of the word. Politics and morality are about public, collective choices. Political and moral concerns include the values, culture and mindset that underpin the overt laws or rules that govern society. Party politics and parliamentary democracy are only a tiny part of politics. Politics is also about much more than "voting" with our consumer power to influence the market, because the market as we know it now cannot provide the security and depth of change that we need: they are currently not for sale.[6]

The rest of this book examines what we can do as we stand in the gap between what is and what might be. It looks at creating the cultural base out of which we might all –citizens and governments – make such moral choices. I treat culture as human intelligence in its broadest sense and I examine how we can develop human capacities for intelligence, which have declined in a modern world that puts such a strong emphasis on a narrowly defined economics.

CHAPTER 8

CITIZEN-LEADERS IN THE MOVEMENT FOR *ENOUGH*

For an ecological, living society and economy, we need overt rules and policies, based on keystone principles and expressed in complementary social institutions and structures (see Chapter 7). We also need certain values, mindset and attitudes, in other words, culture. We wait in hope that our elected leaders and designated lawmakers will make the rules and create the structures we need. With keystone policies in place, we as citizens could follow, and the potential of *enough* could emerge in a co-created way. However, elected leaders, good though their intentions may be when they run for office, and sincere though their commitment to the public good may be when in office, are often forced to plan in the short term and react to current circumstances. Once elected, they frequently fail to show real leadership, because they want to be returned at the next election. They also often lack power to make big changes because they have signed up to agreements with the World Trade Organization (WTO) and large corporations (see Chapter 2).

Since this is the case, ordinary citizens have to take the lead in the movement for *enough*. We cannot make rules or establish security in the very broadest contexts; only government or indeed global government can do that. But as citizens of the earth, we can try to live new ecologically and morally sound cultures into being.[1] We can come together in life-enhancing ways, even if that means going against the grain of many of the structures around us. Culture, which can also be understood as human intelligence in its broadest sense, is of equal importance to social and economic structures. The relationship between culture and law is dynamic and we cannot say which must come first or which is more important; both are essential. Culture and identity are less formal ways of responding to the world than rules or laws, but both the formal and the informal must be present. When we focus on culture, we ask what personal and collective values we need to re-awaken, preserve, or create, while also keeping in mind the rules and policies, and working to influence them.

In the absence of formal public policies based on *enough*, we can all take up the role of citizen-leaders and promote a culture of *enough*. We can draw on keystone attitudes such as stability, creativity, equity and participation (see Chapter 7). We can lead a movement *for* quality, wholeness, sufficiency, well-being, morality, ecology and full human potential. At the same time this movement resists injustice, quantification, monetarism, denial, isolation, cruelty and the deskilling of human beings.

Citizen-leadership

Citizen-leadership is an ecological concept. In an ecological model, everybody follows at some times and everybody takes the lead at some times, depending on what the situation requires. It also includes the ecological idea of wanting to make a contribution, of each individual functioning on behalf of the whole, and, in return, being sustained by the whole. If leadership does not come from one quarter, then it comes from another. There may be a designated or elected leader, but leadership is not confined to that person.

In the modern era, the notion of leader has come to mean that of heroic expert who shows the way. When we think of leadership we often think of our public representatives or desig-nated religious or business leaders. Sometimes we see leadership potential for ourselves as part of our jobs, especially if we work in the public service or in business.

But it is not usual to talk about manual work or so-called low-skilled or low-status jobs in the same breath as leadership. And we rarely think of ourselves as leaders in our off-the-job roles as ordinary citizens.

Citizens in modernist cultures are supposed to think, act and feel in certain ways. We are expected to be endlessly flexible about how we do our jobs and other paid work. We are expected not to ask too many awkward questions and to produce and consume while ignoring many of the consequences of unregulated growth. This kind of citizenship is also about voting, paying taxes, following others or waiting for "them" to lead (how often do we say "they should do something"?). Citizenship in this worldview is not about taking initiative and producing new visions.

We cannot all be official, designated leaders, but if leadership is about taking risks and bringing other people along in a new vision, then we *can* all do it. We need to get rid of the idea that only experts can lead us. A leader is anyone who wants to help[2] and leadership is an everyday thing, not something apart from day-to-day living. It is not confined to those who have decision-making power in institutions or states. We can all, no matter what our age, occupation or role, regularly ask questions about how we should live, what is good, how we can achieve well being for everybody, how we can respect the earth and how we can take the long-term view and try to see the whole picture. We can engage in conversation with others about these issues. A society that does not cultivate the art of asking questions cannot count on finding answers to its most pressing issues.[3]

We may argue that we should not have to take on a leadership role and that we are entitled as ordinary people to just get on quietly with life without having to make the effort of leadership. But the times demand leadership of us, because if we do not lead, who will? We need to respond, like the millions who signed up to fight in the world wars, to do ambulance service or to work at home in factories or on the land. This time the task is at home for all of us, it is open to both sexes and all ages and it concerns cultivating a neglected way of seeing and being in the world, so that we can create positive futures.

The concept of the citizen-leader combines notions of the individual and the collective, the private and the public. Citizens who have concerns about the future can come together in movements to redesign political parties and churches, movements concerning food, transport and time, as well as conversation groups concerned with exploring current events. These are places where people can learn together and support each other in new ways of thinking, as well as actions for change towards security, equity and care.

Citizen-leaders are the source of a vibrant public sphere, where people are willing to become involved in the basic institutions that shape our lives: government, workplace, home and education. In such a democratic public sphere we can talk to and listen to each other, as individuals, communities, nations and states. It is the ground where citizens and government relate to each other. It is also the space where we can ensure that the building of local economies is not taken over by those who want to exclude strangers, cultivate divisions or disregard global security.

Cultivating the middle ground

In the places where citizen-leaders come together, we can promote the idea of the great middle ground. The "middle ground" refers to the masses of people all over the world whose way of living is between over-consumption and poverty; they live without making excessive demands on the earth. It is a materially moderate lifestyle, or culture of permanence, which can reduce stress on the natural environment while also supporting personal and community well-being and which can meet the diverse needs of people throughout the world.[4]

The middle ground is *enough* in action in many different

ways. People living in this middle ground are sustainers. They provide the models we need for sustainable lifestyles: lives rich in rewarding social relations, meaningful work and enjoyable leisure activities but low in waste, energy use and environmental degradation.[5] This middle ground involves healthy food (largely vegetarian but with some meat) and access to clean water. It is a world of rich choices,[6] where people tend to use services instead of buying material products; they use energy and material-intensive goods sparingly; there is a low turnover of consumer goods (they choose durables rather than disposables); and there is little waste to be recycled (in other words, people reduce their consumption and re-use everything they can). There is also substantial personal mobility by convivial means of transport such as bicycles, buses, trains and ferries.[7]

This sustaining model of living is also information-intensive and skill-based. It takes technology very seriously, being neither technophilic or technophobic,[8] but always judging new technology on how it contributes to quality of life. Middle-ground sustainers understand that sometimes it is appropriate to use technology, but that we also need to understand exactly what our needs are before we turn to technology as a solution.

The proposals for Intelligent Agriculture and the frameworks for Contraction and Convergence and a Citizens' Income are about strengthening the middle ground and creating formal opportunities for people to become part of it. Those of us who already identify with and try to live in the middle ground have to push for the change in the rules that would put those or similar proposals in place. Ideally, the process is two-way: governments who have the power to make rules and people who have the power to make culture simultaneously take the initiative. In the absence of the ideal, the sustainers of the middle ground have to take the lead. In this way, our wisdom could educate those who are elected to govern.

Many countries currently contain middle-ground sustainers,

along with rich over-consumers and poor. The rich are a problem because their high consumption involves them in ecological destruction, although indirectly. Most of us in affluent countries are rich and we have to make a considerable effort to avoid harming the world around us. The very poor are also a problem because they are often forced to degrade the environment. They may trigger soil erosion by cultivating marginal ground that would be best left for trees or grazing. For fuel, they are often forced to use valuable trees in the absence of any other fuels.[9] They may be forced to migrate, putting pressure on the resources of others.

In the 1990s, Alan Durning calculated that 3.3 billion of the world population of 5.5 billion belonged to this middle ground, far too many to be dismissed as a middle class (1.1 billion were over-consumers and 1.1 billion were living in poverty).[10] Although large, however, the middle ground is fragile and needs protection and encouragement. Its sheer numbers are not enough to create the changes we need, nor to guarantee its survival. Many people who practice middle-ground values are not consciously part of it. The model of economic growth that dominates globally encourages all to aim for the over-consuming rich group. The values of the middle ground are not sufficiently admired or encouraged.

The grass-roots green movement in Britain is helping people, who are poor by British standards yet affluent by the standards of many majority countries, to identify with the middle ground. Activists are spreading the skills of growing and cooking, re-using many goods and using bicycles for transport. This way of life is an alternative to depending on supermarkets to supply food. It is healthier, so it places fewer demands on public health-services. And it is rewarding. Other examples of movements that support the middle ground are transition-towns, simple living, eco-villages, cycling campaigns, Slow Food, and many more.[11] Several good books, websites and movements can help anybody become a middle-ground sustainer, by starting a personal practice of *enough*.[12]

A huge diversity of lifestyles appears within the middle ground; it provides many models for moral and ecological ways of living. This diversity is significant: it shows that we do not have to be uniform if we want to adapt our behavior in such a way that the planet can renew itself. The task of achieving stability and creating adaptive and dynamic systems is not about making us all live in the same way. It is about participation by as many creative individuals as possible, in systems that support life and well-being. And the common thread is an appreciation of sufficiency, a sense of the richness of *enough*, and a love of the earth and its inhabitants.

The value of the ordinary

The middle ground is made up of ordinary people. Citizen-leaders are ordinary people. The real possibility for positive social change lies with humanity at large, but we do not sufficiently value the ordinary. Modernist culture tends to be contemptuous of the ordinary: we always want to stand out from the crowd, whether it is by "excellence" or celebrity. We are reluctant to define "success" as something that emanates from a life of *enough*. Many of us are preoccupied with things that are very far away (such as distant travel), or very close (we spend hours in therapy), or very spectacular (extraordinary scenery or rare animals or plants), but we spend less and less time on the ordinary stuff of life.

The modern cult of "expert" also goes against the middle ground. Modernity fosters the idea that only experts can be concerned with planning and directing economics and society in any meaningful way. In fact, the so-called experts have got it horribly wrong by any moral or ecological standards. Either that or they are cynical beyond measure.[13] Valuing the ordinary is a step on the road to creating a sustaining middle ground. The ordinary talents of ordinary human beings are far more extraordinary than the apparently outstanding talents of the few.[14] All of us have access to ecological and moral capacities; they are not extraordinary.

To value the ordinary is to take an ecological view; every piece of apparently undistinguished scrubland or hedgerow, every micro-organism is just as valuable in ecological terms as the rare species, or the spectacular landscapes that attract so much attention. When a healthy ecosystem is disturbed or damaged, hundreds of thousands of species (most of them micro-organisms) and trillions of individual organisms self-organize to rebuild.[15] This ecological knowledge shows that every person on the planet is important in the evolution of the new worldview, practices and culture that can support thriving economic and political systems. Every one of us, just like all those tiny organisms, has a part to play in creating such life-enhancing cultures.

The ordinary is an essential part of citizen-leadership for the middle ground. The more different or special we feel, the more difficult it is to identify with, connect to, listen to and respond to the world and to others. At the same time as we are connected, each one of us is separate from other people, but not by virtue of our excellence or celebrity. Letting go of an identity of separateness based on excellence, celebrity, or excess may be a humbling thing to do. But it can also be liberating, because it releases us from cultural pressures to conform. Ordinary is not to be confused with sameness: each one of us is unique in terms of history, personality and tastes. Nor is the ordinary the same as mediocrity, although a culture of specialness would try to persuade us otherwise. Citizen-leadership, the ordinary and the middle ground can be the source of a new and rewarding identity, sustaining for us as individuals and sustaining of the world itself.

The middle ground needs a clear sense of its own value, in the individual and collective senses. Somehow, as citizen-leaders, we have to amplify the attractive identity of the middle ground and the value of the ordinary. We have to get them into public awareness and get people talking about them and seeking others who are interested.[16] This includes providing information, but it is also about building *influence* for the idea. We need the world to pick up on the message of *enough* in a thousand different ways, in all its different expressions, whether in personal or public life.

Redefining wealth: qualitative development

The concept of the middle ground also reclaims and develops repressed knowledge about wealth. We all know that wealth has qualitative aspects, but these are played down in modern growth cultures; the focus is always on money and accumulation. To be wealthy is to drive a car, to fly to faraway places, to own material goods (whose manufacture and transport contribute to poverty and ecological degradation). Any redefinition of wealth requires us to examine very carefully what human needs are, and to direct economic activities toward meeting them. In modernist growth cultures, we are encouraged to accumulate for the sake of it; sometimes human needs are met as a trickle-down effect, sometimes not. Quantity increases, but too much quantity can actually destroy quality. Increasingly, real quality requires that we get away from material goods. This is not to argue against money or material goods, only to insist that they be dethroned as humanity's economic gods and become strictly means to the end of real qualitative development.[17]

Redefining wealth can be challenging, but we have the capacity to recognize qualitative wealth and we can strengthen that capacity. We can take the knowledge even further and create new shared meanings about what wealth is. For example, health is wealth. Our modernist definition of health is usually quite narrow, and refers to individual human beings and the absence of illness, or treating the many illnesses that affect people in modern societies. But health includes that of the soil, of people, of animals, the economy, and the planet as a whole, which is a much higher level of health and wealth than modernity allows for.

The redefining of wealth is also a place where public and private policies can come together. A Citizens' Income (see Chapter 5) represents a public policy of financial security for everyone and is best received when individual citizens have an appreciation of *enough*, and where the cultural milieu values *enough*. The value of carbon quotas (see Chapter 4) comes from recognizing the wealth inherent in nature. Currently, we see wealth in terms of activities and possessions that are carbon profligate. But if we accept the need for carbon capping, and accept the notions of fair quotas per capita along with quota trading, then carbon-thrifty people and nations are wealthy.

Qualitative approaches to wealth break the links between material consumption and well-being. It is stressful to have too many things. We have to maintain them and protect them and we may feel guilty if we do not use them. Consuming too much also lessens our humanity. An emphasis on material wealth cuts us off from knowledge of self, of who we are without those things we buy. Consuming can sometimes be a way to anaesthetize ourselves against feelings of depression, boredom, despair or exhaustion. It adds to our alienation, that is, the way we feel when there is little to define the self apart from paid work, income and possessions. *Enough* can help us find out who we are when we define ourselves in other ways apart from material and quantitative wealth. Deep self-knowledge is a form of wealth that is not encouraged within our current power arrangements.

Good traditions are also a form of wealth; they are like seed varieties that we may need in the future.[18] It would also be wise to restore the kinds of knowledge that were once valued and to respect them where they still exist. If we look closely enough, we can see many kinds of wealth in the world around us, such as the beauty and elegance of frugality and simplicity. But within growth societies, valuing this kind of qualitative wealth is often seen as an idiosyncratic or irrational rejection or criticism of affluence. Alternatively, it may be associated with those who cannot "make it" in conventional terms of success.

Social wealth

Qualitative wealth includes social wealth: belonging to a network of relationships and communities. We have an innate connectedness with other living beings and with nature, which is part of social wealth but which we often do not recognize. Computers can connect us to each other, and can be truly a tool for conviviality. But they also offer a disembodied form of connectivity that denies physicality, compresses emotions through a cognitive prism, cushions us from direct experience of others and the outdoors and ignores spirituality.[19] We ought not to become dependent on them for connections. It would be wise to recognize the ways that we are already connected, by virtue of our humanity, to each other, to the planet and to all living things on the planet.

Developing social wealth requires that we go beyond modernist ideas about what constitutes strong civil society. Civil society is all the activities, people and groups that exist outside of government and the money markets. It is a hard-to-define mixture of family, friendship groups, small organizations, churches, community involvement and volunteers. When governments in present-day affluent countries talk about the need to create strong civil societies, they want to encourage networks and relationships that help people to cope well with the demands of daily life. But they usually fail to take into account the deep connections with place and with the land that were present in traditional societies that also had strong social bonds.[20] Modern institutions like the state can be bad at "doing complexity"; they seek just the measurable aspects of strong civil societies and try to re-create them without appreciating the more qualitative aspects.

Part of the leadership we need now has to be about reclaiming and identifying some of the human capacities for connection that modernity has stunted. In an ecological way of thinking, the individual is hugely important. Ecology values the collective wisdom of whole systems, but does not ignore the individuality of each person and the unique nature of each person's relationship to the world. In this way of thinking, connection is wealth. A sense of connectedness to the world takes us from the isolation of discrete individuals to a sense of the person as part of a larger system. It is about being part of a group or of a community, but without feeling obliged to conform. We can retain our individuality and uniqueness within a system where the different parts stimulate each other and imagination can emerge, flourish and circulate.

Power and imagination

To encourage attitudes of the middle ground, everyday citizen-leadership and valuing the ordinary is not as straightforward as it sounds. The limited collective choices currently available to us have served to narrow our individual, institutional and community imaginations and intelligence. Our discernment is blunted when it comes to recognizing what makes a good, satisfying life of well being.[21] In other words, the choices currently offered to us have narrowed our culture.

Culture is the filter for information; we have a great deal of information about our situation, which is wonderful, but the culture does not provide a fertile ground for creative use of that information. Information is channeled so that an everyday consensus emerges, namely, that economic growth is the only game in town worth pursuing. The power of this consensus is so great that it largely shapes the ways we think, behave and regulate ourselves. It creates our visions of what life can be. The consensus ignores other forms of economic activity and development comes to mean increase in GDP. A leader has to work to expose other realities, such the biological reality of our dependence on nature, along with the existence of limits and moral considerations. We need to have visions that are informed by the widest possible definition of the knowledge economy. Then we can use our learning in the service of human well-being and the common good.

Power works in subtle ways to shape the meanings we hold about reality and the world around us. The result is that many of us do not have a vocabulary adequate to discuss the issues of our day. This power is built into our lives in ways that are neither accidental nor random. Modernity and its economic systems need us to believe in the knowledge economy in a very narrow sense. They understand knowledge (whether that knowledge is practical, interpersonal, intrapersonal or reflective) and the human capacity to learn as instruments to create money.

Emphasizing the more subtle workings of power over our visions for a good life is not to discount the importance of more overt power or influence. Nor is it to ignore physical violence, hunger or disease. But it is to say that current economic and political systems have huge power over our imaginations; they shape the ways we think about the future and how we might create something different from the dominant system. Social, economic and political forces, which on the face of it have nothing to do with our personal beliefs and experiences, have far more power over us than we may realize. They influence the way we understand the world and how we feel about it. Such power, though invisible, has enormous effects.

When we become aware of power so subtle that many do not see it, it can be tempting to succumb to despair. The only way to overcome despair is to resist. Only if we become increasingly aware of the resistance of others and resist ourselves can we regain the sense of peace that necessarily leaves us when we end our own flight from reality.[22] Our capacity to resist and to join with others in resistance is a huge resource. Yet, resistance is not always about going head-on against the prevailing system. Resistance is also about creating a cultural tipping point in favor of morality and ecology by means of creativity, imagination and passion.

History

A more complex understanding of history would also help us to have faith in our capacity to develop positive cultures for the future. Knowing about the historical period in which we live right now is of course essential so that we can work out how to proceed. But we also need a more complex sense of the past, so that we understand it as one where there were different possibilities. The versions of modernity and economics that emerged were not inevitable, and many people struggled against quantification, monetarism, alienation and other ways of reducing humans to units of production.

The quest for a more humane approach to life, similar to that of the middle ground, is part of a significant and substantial tradition, which challenges the most alienating aspects of modernist culture. Included are the Romantic movement, the Arts and Crafts movement, the cosmological and spiritual quests in schools of painting, the counter-modern Modernists, the work of Mahatma Gandhi and the counterculture of the 1960s and early 1970s. These movements, like the movement for *enough*, were about re-humanizing culture and ways of living, in societies that were embracing modernity in the form of industrialism, individualism and the pursuit of profit.[23]

In creating new visions that centre on *enough*, we can participate to some extent in our own evolution, choosing moral and ecological paths, and turning away from paths where material, quantitative wealth is valued over all else. Evolution here means, not the ceaseless flexibility and adaptation demanded by growth economics, but a bringing together of the forces of nature and culture in a developmental spiral. Human history can no longer be seen as separate and different from biological evolution, but as the social evolution of one species within the web of life on earth. One of the best metaphors for the coming together of nature and culture is the story; we humans can tell ourselves stories about how the world can be and about how we can be.[24]

New stories about change

Modernist culture needs us to think of constant change, imposed from outside us, as a supreme good. Most change available to us, however, is just producing more of the same, more ways of conforming to the dominant mindset and lifestyles. Change comes to mean more of the modern, only speeded up into a hypermodern way of living that is actually boring and deadening. Change of this kind creates great stress, but a growth mentality tells us that we must adapt to it or get left behind. It wants us to deride those who are cautious about that kind of change, portraying us as backward traditionalists. Moral, ecological and aesthetic stories are lost in this culture of constant change, much of it based on the market: whatever the market will support is acceptable. (See also Chapter 2 on monetarism.)

As I write this paragraph in early 2009, we appear to be at a crossroads. The banking crisis and world recession are beginning to bite and the G20 states have met in New York to plan a response. Food crises are also on the agenda, although not as strongly. Global warming has gone down on the list of priorities and social justice is rarely mentioned. Still, many commentators note how this crisis is an opportunity for our designated leaders to create a new world order, since the deep illnesses of capitalism have been revealed.the logic of economic growth at all costs, which has for a long time been held up as gospel, is more open to challenge than in the past. NGOs and organizations for an alternative economics are of course making all the connections, but the signs so far are that the G20 leaders simply want to re-create the old system; their visions seem terribly narrow.

We need a much bigger vision of change, progress and advancement. There are far more exciting and dynamic options than the vision offered by modernity. We need to understand and emphasize the value of cyclical and organic change. Certain systems need to die so that others can grow. Intelligent Agriculture, Citizens' Income and Contraction and Convergence are about genuine change that takes us away from more of the same. And the culture we are trying to develop is also a kind of framework to take us into a different kind of thinking and different ways to know the world. We can develop the ability to understand and consciously evolve our worldview. We can also tell ourselves stories of what the future could be like, but without shying away from the pain of the present. And if our designated and elected leaders are not doing this, citizens have to take the lead. A strong movement of citizen-leaders has to try to negotiate with and influence the official leaders at global and local levels.

The movement of citizen-leaders of the middle ground for planetary and human well-being is counter-cultural, and that makes it difficult. Leaders (all of us) need emotional strength, depth of vision and capacity for both self-reflection and a more distanced overview of the world. Intellectually, we may be able to accept the idea of citizen-leadership and the middle ground. But this kind of leadership also takes persistence, quiet courage, patience and a willingness to take risks, in uncertain circumstances over a prolonged period; then when the big choices come, we can be ready for them. It also means having contact with others who are of like mind.

The notion of practice is important here. With practice, you can improve almost anything: your social skills, your tennis serve, your muscle strength or flexibility. You work at your edges all the time to extend your comfort zone a bit. We all encounter moral challenges every day. We need to recognize these challenges for what they are and use *enough* to guide our responses. No matter how small the choices, they are important. They help us to acquire a sort of "morality fitness"; we cannot make the big moral choices if we do not make the small ones too. This is everyday leadership.[25] And it can percolate through to national and big-system levels. After a number of inhabitants of a system have learned a certain behavior, others of the same species are able to learn that behavior more easily.[26]

Leading the movement of *enough* is about participating in the world creatively and lovingly.[27] The next chapter continues the theme of this one, and examines inner work for citizen-leaders. Contemplation and a turn inward are essential activities for all, if we are to make sure that the external world of economic activity is of a kind that serves us well.

CHAPTER 9

OUR WORLD, OUR SELVES

The present moment requires citizen-leaders who can act publicly in the world with protectiveness and vigilance towards it.[1] To do so most effectively requires that we also restore lost qualities of humanity, which have withered through lack of use in modern life, but which are an important part of full participation in the world. We can reconnect with a substantial tradition that values feeling, care, relationship, mystery and silence, along with the action and the abstract thinking favored by modernity. The inner life of mind and heart is inextricable from the outer life of action and service, citizenship and leadership. Inner and outer experiences depend on each other and create each other; both kinds are essential for a full humanity.

The modern world would have us ignore certain social and economic information and distance ourselves from and deny the consequences of our actions for other humans, for the earth and other living beings. Equally, the education and development of the modern person ignore important capacities of the self. Modernity confines us in a state that is far less than what we might be, but we can learn to transcend this state and rebuild human intelligence in its broadest sense. The intellect, to work at its best, has to be multiple and has to cultivate many ways of knowing. Each person can know through the body, through feelings, through concept-forming, rational description and simply being, and all of these ways of knowing are equal in value. In order to reclaim the less-developed capacities, we have to go within. The inner journey is about recognising deeper levels within ourselves and between ourselves and the world, just as spirituality, morality and ecology recognise those levels also (see Chapter 1).[2] If we engage in inner work, our outer work is deepened and more sustainable, and our responses of outer action can be as appropriate as possible for each situation. The journey within does not involve psychological therapy, amateur or otherwise, although the journey is often therapeutic, and good therapy can also be a part of the journey within.

Modernity encourages us to see ourselves as divorced from the world around us, or, more accurately, to see the world as something that *surrounds* us, not something that is *in* us.

In modern life, we suffer from overload of information; there are numerous demands on our time; we are surrounded by people, with most of whom we cannot create meaningful relationships. The emotional demands on us are legion. We lack time and space, essential resources for cultivating deep understandings and contemplating meaning. We are encouraged to deal with this by cultivating a discrete self, which seeks possession of material things, of facts or of more information.[3]

The emphasis on the discrete self and its separateness from the world prevents us from developing an ecological understanding of humans as part of the world. The discrete self could be understood as minimal. But the self also exists at other levels: that of relationship and that of union with the world, flowing or dancing in it. The relational self knows and thrives on interconnection and interdependence. The dancing self appreciates mystery and other experiences and ways of knowing that often do not lend themselves to rational description. The dancing self knows how to limit or stop thought, how to be still and slow and simply to experience the world or the present moment, without trying to name or rationalise the experience.[4]

The three levels of self – discrete, relational and dancing - are intimately interconnected and bring together the physical, emotional, spiritual and mental aspects of our being. The original meaning of the word "individual" refers to someone who is whole, whose self is not divided into separate parts.[5] But we let the discrete self dominate, most of the time. We give some (although weak) attention to the relational self, and we tend to ignore the dancing self completely.

The capacity to think

The inner journey for most moderns will probably start with thinking. Our capacity to rationally understand and critique is valuable, because we need to have information about world social, economic and political events and to apply moral and ecological standards of judgement to them. Modernity offers us a certain kind of thinking, which emphasizes rational debate, which in turn emphasizes the discrete self's capacities to process information cognitively and reach considered decisions. This kind of thinking is important and the dangers of not doing it are immense. Avoidance, ignorance and denial of real problems come about because of not thinking fully or by not thinking at all.

Morality, ecology, health, well-being, wealth, sustainability, happiness and justice can be cognitively understood in minutes. But that is a minimal understanding; it can take a lifetime to understand them with all our senses and levels of self. Given this, thinking cannot be reduced to a conscious, cognitive process but also needs to include, in every instance, awareness and practice of other ways of knowing. A full rationality incorporates feeling, bodily knowledge and intuitive knowledge; it draws on the multiple capacities of the person.

The capacity to feel

The capacity to feel deeply is an essential resource for enhancing our moral and ecological sensitivity. Feelings can move us to actions that can break taken-for-granted patterns of abuse of the earth and its inhabitants, actions that can start creating humane cultures. If we do not cultivate this capacity, we are separated from a huge part of ourselves and from others and we will find it difficult to cultivate our relational selves.

Feelings and emotions come about when we allow our bodies to respond to and co-operate with an image, a thought or a memory.[6] I use the terms feeling and emotion interchangeably here, although social convention in English frequently downgrades words associated with emotion, such as "emotive" or "emotional", using them to mean overcome or overwhelmed, and therefore irrational and not to be taken seriously. But thinking and feeling are intimately connected. Feeling is not just the dualistic opposite to thinking; it involves imagination, sensate knowledge, and emotional intelligence, that is, being aware of the feelings and emotions that are occurring for oneself and sensitive to those of others in any particular time or situation.

Our gut feelings of doubt, fear, shame and good sense are among the most valuable ways of knowing that humans have. Even without extensive facts and information at our disposal, our intuitions can often be a guide to critical insights about the world around us.

And when we have many options, feelings and emotions can guide decision-making, because in a multi-option world it is not possible to methodically sift through all options. Feeling knowledge can be a reliable guide to making choices.

Feeling is not superior to thinking, nor is an emphasis on it a reason to reduce feeling to process or ritual, both of which can become substitutes for feeling deeply and thinking critically. Reason flows from the blending of rational thought and feeling. If the two functions are torn apart, thinking deteriorates into schizoid intellectual activity and feeling deteriorates into neurotic life-damaging passions.[7] While feeling has a part to play in how we think beyond modernity's limited version of ratio-nality, thinking has a part to play in becoming aware of what we are feeling.

Our bodies can also help us to recognize feelings. In order to feel deeply, we need to reclaim a sense of the human body, different from the one promoted in advertising, separate from the trappings of commodities, fashion and being cool. We often fail to become aware of our feelings partly because we have lost a sense of the body as a source of knowledge. If one is uncertain of what it is one is feeling, thinking may not help and bodily sensations can be a guide. We can also learn that other people's bodies are similarly fragile and a source of feeling; the body is something we all have in common.[8]

The focus here on a conscious awareness of feelings does not deny the unconscious, nor does it imply that there are no unconscious forces leading us to feel as we do. But the kind of awareness of feelings that I wish to pursue takes as a starting point a person's own definition of a feeling.[9]

Feelings are also culturally guided and shaped. People in different social and physical worlds experience feelings differently. If you are oppressed or disadvantaged, you will have a different emotional environment from that of someone who is powerfully positioned in society.[10] Societal patterns for feeling and emotion also show up in differences between how women and men experience them. In general, modern men learn to deny feelings. It is socially required for men who acquire positions of authority in public life to be rational in a very particular way: distanced, objective, logical, aggressive and autonomous. In other words, they are supposed to cultivate their discrete selves, play down their relational and dancing selves and suppress emotional reactions to events and to the consequences of their actions. Those women who "make it" in public life or positions of authority are often expected to fit this model.

We should be careful about accepting at face value the images that men and some women project of themselves as unemotional; feelings exist for everyone, and some leaders do acknowledge them. But it is generally accepted that to show emotion in public life is to lose control and authority. Although public life and public institutions are designed to run as if feelings did not exist, it is more the case that feelings are present but not acknowledged. In fact, repressed or unacknowledged feelings can have strong effects. And repressed pain or grief can become quiet depression or numbness of spirit.[11]

Pain

Modern societies put a lot of energy into avoiding emotional pain and denying that anything is wrong. Denial is a very short-term survival function; it operates on a social and individual basis to allow us ignore contradictions, ambivalence or doubt. Perhaps we deny pain because we fear it. If we admit to it, it may break us apart and put us in touch with our doubts and uncertainties. Pain and nothingness are frequently unspoken feelings about the world around us. Grief, fear and despair are often ignored or suppressed, but at the same time are important ways of learning and knowing.

Those of us who deny it need to recover our capacity to acknowledge pain. Pain keeps us alert to wrong and makes us connect with others who feel pain. We need to feel the pain of those who are dispossessed, oppressed and abused, who are denied dignity or who lose dignity. We need to feel pain as the world is damaged, as violence is done to nature. Many ecologically and morally aware people speak of the pain they felt on seeing significant outdoor places from their childhood violated by building or other "development". These were not spectacular places, but ordinary patches of ground where nature flourished and children played.

Biologically, pain is a message that something is wrong and it stimulates us to avoid or change the dangerous situation. Emotionally, we need to act on the same cues. Pain may tear us apart, but at the same time it can lead us to something new. The ability to recognize and act on pain is essential for creativity and wholeness and is a first step in breaking though denial, into compassion and an ability to take action for change. We need to acknowledge pain and look into its sources, rather than displacing it with work, spending, sport, individual success, drugs, over-eating or not eating, self-harming, computer games, television, even with patriotism and war.[12]

Anger is often a cover for grief, which comes about following death and loss. And many of us have lost a great deal in the project of modernity: our habitat, connections to the land, meaningful work and meaningful communities. But denial of this kind of death is a striking part of the modernist worldview. And at the same time, we accept as "reality" certain kinds of death and destruction: of people, animals and natural systems from pollution or war. We accept that cancer is ever-present, due to environmental pollution, contaminated water and toxic food.

A society in a state of denial looks quite normal to us; denial is how we construct a superficial form of sanity for ourselves in the midst of the not-so-nice consequences of many of our economic actions.[13] But this is a false sanity, ignorant in the sense that it ignores what is going on, uniform in that we just do what everybody does and continue with "business as usual".

The cycles of birth and death are part of an ecological worldview. Everything in nature eventually dies. We are the animal that knows this will happen to us.[14] In this light, what does it matter how much we accomplish or how successful we are? It is more appropriate to ask who we are. We don't have forever. To live every day as if it were one's last can show us what we really value; it can show us how to live. It also shows us that, ultimately, we do not have control over our lives. But we deny this kind of death and do our best to keep it from view in modern life.

We could take the view that since each individual will die, it does not matter if the world is in a worse state when one is gone. Only if we have a sense of belonging and connectedness with other living beings on the planet will we care about what will happen to the planet after our death. The citizen-leader has to do the inner work concerning death, to reflect on the centrality of death in nature and in the cycle of life, in order to gain strength to resist the kinds of death that are wrong. We need to cultivate the capacity to sit with powerful feelings of chaos, despair, grief and darkness; we also need to learn when it is appropriate to resist death and darkness.

Fear

One feeling that *is* routinely cultivated in modern societies is fear. A certain type of fear is essential, if citizens are to acquiesce to the working, earning and spending demands of the global growth economy. We fear that our children may be disadvantaged in the system if they don't have the latest computers, clothing or toys, so we spend in order to "protect" them. Insurance companies spend millions on advertising and many people have come to believe that we have to cushion ourselves with insurance against every possible eventuality. We understandably fear letting our children walk or cycle, we even fear doing so ourselves, because the traffic environment is dangerous. So we come to think of cars as essential for protection. In a vicious circle, more cars make the roads and streets even more dangerous and make it impossible for public transport to operate to schedule.

Insecurity in the wider system shows up as defensiveness in individuals. In this scenario, new things to insure and new possessions to defend keep us constantly worrying and we can never envisage a point of sufficient security. Fear motivates much spending, because we think that buying products and services will give us an edge over others and provide security. But when we have to spend, we have to earn and that means connection to work that may have serious personal, ecological or social consequences.

We also fear uncertainty. We cannot bear for our public representatives to show doubt, considering it a demonstration of powerlessness. Our culture encourages instant action in response to difficulties, and, failing action, it wants rejection. And yet the capacity to hold uncertainty is essential for leaders of all kinds, including citizen-leaders, parents, lawmakers, religious leaders and educators. The capacities of not acting, of waiting, and of patience can create a period of time in which the tensions of not knowing resolve themselves, in order for new possibilities to emerge. But for the most part, we fear to show uncertainty.

Fear is also connected with denial of death. Because we are so detached from nature, we have lost the understanding that all things must die in due course and that this is entirely necessary, in order to make way for the new. But we often cling to old ways, trying to revive projects, systems and ways of thinking that have outlived their value. We consider it failure (which could be seen as a type of death) if we cannot make them continue indefinitely.

We fear failure and in order not to fail, we create a drive for "excellence". If we had a stronger cultural awareness of emotion, we might reject the ways that repressed feeling can be trained or directed into a desire to be better than others. We are trained to disdain the ordinary to such an extent that it is seen as a type of failure. Our cult of celebrity is another expression of this. This fear and its translation into a desire for excellence are more socially acceptable than the anger that sometimes masks fear and other types of pain. But they are no less destructive in the long run.

Often, we repress good-sense reactions, because we experience a need to fit in with what "everybody knows". We fear that if we truly show our feelings of doubt about something, we will be dismissed as old-fashioned, uncool, or unsophisticated. And the denial of those around us often reinforces our own denial of doubt. But what is it to be cool or sophisticated? It can mean keeping certain knowledge under control or out of sight, dismissing our feelings of identification with others, training our emotions in the direction of indifference, putting on a cynical outer skin and fitting in with the dominant culture around us.

Even when we do know what is going on as a result of our consumptive system of growth, our sympathy for others is depleted partly because we fear what might happen to our things and our lifestyles. We might have to give them up, if we felt deeply about the situation and acted on our feelings.

Modern selves are encouraged to be fearful in the face of many small things and to try to control them. At the same time we are supposed to be fearless in the face of the very real and damaging consequences of growth economics. We need a different quality to our fear, that is, to fear what may happen to the earth, our home, as a result of human activity. We may have some rational awareness of what may happen, but by and large we do not feel it deeply. The absence of a visceral and heartfelt fear makes our visions narrow and detaches us from our intuition. We lose our capacity for deep reflection; we concentrate on controlling the small things around us and ignore the big picture. And this shuts us off from a great deal of our potential to be citizen-leaders.

We need deep security and stability in our world, not control. Deep security (in external forms like climate, finance, water and food and in inner forms such as friendship, caring and listening) helps us to cope with the emotional impact of not being able to predict or direct our futures. Letting go of the desire for control is essential if we are to move out of our modernist fears and acknowledge a fear that is an important signal for change. We do not need to let this latter kind of fear paralyze us, but if we acknowledge it, it can prompt us to work with other people for change. And while this very real and worthy kind of fear makes us think of the future, it is also about the present, because to address it, we need to ask, how, right now, we can start to do something about it.

Shame

The modern, discrete self is also encouraged to abandon any feelings of shame. But morality requires a suitably developed sense of shame, so that we refrain from doing harm to other living beings. When shame is wrongly induced, it is important that people be enabled to break free of it, and recent times have seen us leave behind much inappropriate shame about the body, sexuality, family, race, ethnicity, ability and social class. But at the same time, shame is forced on millions of children and adults from non-modern communities. They are made to feel deficient because they do not have the possessions and way of life that affluent minority-world people have.

Shame and associated guilt can have a healthy social function, however. In affluent societies, we need more of them, because they can help us to recognize things that are morally wrong. We are far too inclined to be proud of things of which we should be ashamed. We may be dynamic, energetic and go-getting, but we ought to face up to the consequences of our everyday economic actions on the social and environmental stage, even if governments tell us there is no alternative. We need to develop our capacity for shame and guilt in ways that will help us overcome our fears of looking stupid, of not fitting in, or of losing our way of life. Thus, we can build our capacity for functioning in terms of reciprocity, responsibility, obligation, sympathy, and trust, important capacities in building community and solidarity. Those capacities are in us, although underused and underdeveloped. Shame and guilt can lead us to them.

Contemplating dependency

In modern societies, we have come to understand dependency as shameful. The discrete self is encouraged to deny its dependency on others, and on the natural resources of the earth. We are to be individualistic, self-sufficient, and in control. This is a superficial independence, yet it isolates us profoundly from the needs of our fellow humans and from other living things. The tendency of modernity is to minimize the range of need that human beings have and to regard as weak those who display more needs than others. Yet, ironically, in the big picture, global capitalism requires us in our nation-states to be dependent on large corporations and their ability to create money and move it around the globe.

To develop the relational and dancing levels of self, we need to embrace our innate ecological dependency, which is a source of connection with other people and with the world. Far from preventing our freedom, dependency, in its ecological sense, can show us how to be fully human. Appreciation of dependency makes us aware of needs; deep stability is founded on sensitivity to the most profound needs of humans and the earth.

Understanding one's own dependency can provide pointers about how to help another person. It can teach us to give care without characterizing others as helpless or making them feel shame or guilt at receiving our time or resources. It is about relating to someone else as an equal. The discrete self learns to compete with and compare itself to others, while the relational self learns to accept its own dependency and to accompany others in theirs.

Care

Each person has the capacity to care about and to give care to other people and for the earth. Caring *about* is central to morality. It is a passion inside you, for earth, people and animals.[15] If we all truly cared enough, everything would be okay, and we would give care, which is the practical expression of caring about. While the two forms of care are distinct, they are also intimately linked. Because if one cares enough about something or somebody, one will do one's best to give care, to put care into practice. If we cared enough about food security, health, social justice and natural systems, we would not engage in industrial farming, for example. If we had enough passion, everything would work itself out. Many young people are passionate, but the modern culture in which they find themselves most often relies on information as a way to tackle problems. It appeals to the discrete self.

Modernity encourages us to care only about our intimates, those closest to us, usually lovers or members of our nuclear families. It discourages care about or for those who are strangers to us. In fact, it cultivates indifference, which is an emotional state that prevents any kind of action to improve the world, to take a moral position, or to fight against injustice. Indifference is incompatible with citizen-leadership and is probably the most dangerous emotional state of all. Care is the direct opposite of indifference. Although neglected in modernity, care has never died out in modern societies and it is having a resurgence: many people who find themselves living in modernity are resisting the cultural imperatives to be indifferent. Those who are cultivating and encouraging care are already engaging in citizen-leadership for a new culture.

Both kinds of care involve empathy and identification with our own and others' needs, even with their suffering. Care is "the work that mother used to do".[16] But new forms of care, like the philosophy and practice of *enough*, are not just about going back to past ways. They involve developing a different approach, which, in particular, gets men involved and increases the supply of care in society, without putting extra burdens on women. We put time, feeling, actions and contemplation into care, drawing on all levels of self. Care (especially actively giving care, or care *of*) is a form of work, and, like all forms of work, is one of the chief means we have of engaging with and relating to the world. (See also Chapters 2 and 5 on work.)

Care is both a capacity and a need. Each one of us also has a need to receive care, but many of us find it hard to accept care from others (some find it easier if they are paying for it). Sometimes, as moderns, we give charity rather than care to others, whom we consider unequal to us. Or we think we can "give" progress and development to non-moderns. Sometimes, we take things that sustain us from others or from the earth in an unjust manner, but refuse to see ourselves as takers. Rarely do we reflect on what it means to give care in a spirit of equality, or to receive it in a similar manner. Receiving has to be distinguished from taking.[17]

We also need to understand care in its fullest sense. In modern life, we may provide physical care but people are largely encouraged to manage their own emotional needs in an independent fashion. We have reduced the range of what someone needs, by encouraging an ideal model of the person as independent and discrete. Modernity recognises only minimal aspects of care and then puts them into the realm of the market and cash economies; in other words, modernity commercialises care. When something is commercialised, it becomes practical, "efficient" and rational but downplays the need for patient, relational engagement. A full range of care can be slow, and therefore inefficient and not always compatible with the commercial world.[18]

We often neglect a full range of self-care too; yet a full humanity requires that we take care of our own bodies, minds and hearts. Citizen-leaders need personal energy and deep personal stability, so that they can play their part in creating a new culture and actions to care for the world. Their well-being is a form of wealth. In the modern world, rest and self-care are radical acts. If we do not understand these issues in ourselves, we will not be able to act as citizen-leaders and put care and love into practice with the world or with other people. When we experience being cared for and caring for ourselves in a full manner, we recognize this fullness and usually value it. We have to experience something only once, to know its possibility and its absence in our lives.[19]

Love is an essential feeling resource for care and being

together in our dependency. We need more of the kind of love that involves strangers. We have come to think of love as largely a private emotion for another individual.[20] Many people find it initially awkward to talk about love in a more public and communal context, because we have individualised and privatised love and care. In this context, we think it appropriate that only intimates provide care for each other. We often expect one other person who is close to us to meet all our needs, whether physical or emotional. This puts huge expectations and demands, often impossible to fulfil, on individuals.

We need to communise love and to see it as having multiple forms (so this does not rule out individual, private love, but it distributes the burden of expectation). We need enough of all the different kinds of love.[21] Empathy, friendship, kindness, identification and solidarity are resources for bridging the gap between public love and private love. They also form the basis for moral development.

Listening

One way we can develop our capacity for care, love, kindness and friendship – private and communal – is by a disciplined listening to other people and the world around us. Listening to other people and the world also involves observing them and turning towards them, instead of isolating ourselves as modern culture would encourage us to do. As listeners and observers we also can learn about ourselves, our different levels of self, and about self in the world. Listening is love and care in action. The sane prefer listening to speaking; indeed they regard most speaking as a defense against listening, although they realize what could happen if everyone wanted only to listen. [22] The relational and dancing selves are more inclined than the discrete self to listen.

Listening is probably the hardest, most disciplined, most profound and most important work of leadership.[23] It is a huge challenge to us moderns. The discrete self likes to speak, because to truly listen is to risk being changed. What I have learned about listening may seem naïve. But it is a hugely sophisticated activity, although its principles are devastatingly simple. Listening is actually innocence and sophistication combined, in a way that goes beyond either. It is a way of giving to other people and to the world, based on a belief that something is beautiful and worth doing, because it is right.[24]

It is a discipline that involves a clear intent, asking oneself all the time, "why am I doing this and what is its purpose?" Listening is a commitment, and commitment requires persistence and perseverance, even though the outcome cannot be known. If one knows the outcome, it does not require a commitment. What makes it a commitment is the fact that you do not know how it will turn out yet you do it anyway. You risk being changed. You draw on past experience, desire in the present and a faith in the future.

Many people such as therapists or spiritual advisors are already expert listeners. This is a very individualized and private form of listening, although it is valuable for ordinary people too to practice it in everyday relationships and in one-to-one situations. But to really develop listening as a leadership activity for communal love, care and friendship, we need to take it into community.

Listening in community is how we do inner work together and how we bring love and care out of the purely private and individual domains and into the domain of public life. It is an essential key for how we move forward and at the same time participate in our own evolution as moral and ecological humans. A listening community can be a small group of people who come together with the express purpose of supporting each other by listening. This can be in the workplace, family, household, church, neighbourhood, parliament, nation, state, global politics or any aspect of life.

Listening does not leap to fix, save or offer charity; it neither invades nor evades. It never involves efforts to persuade or dissuade one another. It involves asking open, honest questions of the person to whom we are listening. People who listen to each other well in community do so in a spirit of equality. It allows each person who is speaking to hold uncertainty and the tensions of not knowing, for as long as it takes to come to some kind of insight. It also protects a safe space for diverse views and experiences.[25] In this way, listening honors the individuality and discreteness of each person, but helps them to develop their relational and dancing selves at the same time. It uses community to strengthen the self, and simultaneously develops each person's capacity for community. It involves the paradox of having relationships in which we protect each other's aloneness.[26]

When we listen and are heard in community, it activates wisdom; something emerges that we cannot predict. Through community listening, one can also learn to listen to oneself, to one's moral judgment, to one's emotions. This takes us beyond denial or the self-protection that is so often the response of the discrete self. This kind of listening also has a spiritual dimension, requiring that both speaker and listener stay in the present moment. In that sense, it can activate the dancing self. It is not the same as being passive or resigned. It is presence and awareness, without trying to impose one's opinions or act.

Uncertainty and mystery

We need to understand the value of not knowing, even as we engage our discrete and relational selves in an intellectual, spiritual and emotional search for meaning and moral judgement. The decline of meaning in hypermodern societies can give life to new meaning and a new worldview. However, meaning, while it is hugely important to us and we want to create it, is not something that we can fully possess. It is a matter of how my existence figures in the world, and in the lives of others; one can never grasp this completely. Genuine meaningfulness always contains an absence as well as a presence, silence as much as declaration.[27] Wealth also resides in not having, in letting go, in relinquishing the grasping for certainty. This takes us way beyond modernist formulations of meaning and wealth and into the value of ways of knowing that are about not thinking or feeling, but about stilling the mind and pure *being* in the moment.

Science, art and religion can help us develop an appreciation of the mystery in all reality and allow us to respectfully reach out to this mystery. Embracing mystery is moving into a field of forces that is in fact one's deepest self and it can show us our deepest connections. We can go on to make rational choices for action, based on those connections. However, even as we act, we have to acknowledge that to understand perfectly is to misunderstand completely. To have everything "perfectly under control" is to be under the greatest of illusions. "Confusion, acknowledged, is a virtue".[28] Paradox can lead us to wisdom; opposites do not necessarily negate each other. We have to go regularly into the unspoken and leave space for the liminal, the marginal, the unconscious and the embodied. We need time and mental space for stillness, for mystery and for learning from our feelings of ambivalence or contradictions.

The citizen-leader will benefit from cultivating all three selves. Along with building up the capacities for inner work, including capacities for feeling and mystery, we can also develop an intellectual appreciation of the inner journey. We need to give the inner life a courageous, rational and informed defence in the world today. Too often the people who advocate it put forward seemingly outrageous expressions of it, without understanding its foundations. This results in a very bad press for inner work, and allows it to be easily ridiculed and dismissed.

I am not advocating some abstract standard for the human

person, in the search for *enough*. But I am saying that without the inner work, the outer work suffers. The inner journey needs to exist on an equal footing with the outer journey of information, facts and rational thought. We don't need to elevate one over the other, but to hold both in creative tension and allow the inner and outer work to inform each other. All the capacities that are undervalued in modernity are nevertheless within us. We just need to exercise them – even in small ways – and build a sufficiency of them in the world.

CONCLUSION

I started this book in 2006, when many countries were experiencing a major economic boom and very few people took seriously global warming, food security or the injustice caused by deregulated financial markets. I finished it in early 2009, when there was much wider recognition of what was happening. At this time too the global financial crisis has highlighted the importance of the state, along with international governance, in creating boundaries and regulations. Although the deregulation of markets has been the main agenda since the 1980s, increasing numbers of people are now calling for global rules, principles and regulations for the financial markets. If such large numbers of people can call for governance for the financial markets, the call can be amplified also for climate and food security and for the social justice that would be a spin-off from that type of security. The regulation we require needs to be based on solid moral and ecological principles.

There are, then, signs that things could change radically. But the change could go either way. The crises we are experiencing could equally result in calls for closing borders and the end to international aid and cooperation. They could be a signal for divisive and chauvinistic elements in society to blame strangers or outsiders for problems and to foster fear and suspicion. We must strive for the best aspects of humanity to prevail so that we can combine the best of globalisation – an appreciation of cultural diversity, a recognition of our common humanity, solidarity with others all over the world and the circulation of good ideas – with a desire to build strong and self-reliant local economies.

This book is almost finished now. What remains is the opportunity to continue on the path of morality and ecology. As a global species, we humans still have one foot on a path where asking the question, "what is enough?" is seen as naïve, ridiculously idealistic, or even heretical in the face of the gods of money and unregulated economic growth. But the other foot is already on a path where people are working to establish *enough*. This path is a little faint but nonetheless recognizable. Many people know that it can lead us to a future of elegant, sustainable sufficiency, security and well being for all, rather than poverty for some and short-term affluence for others. Let us take on the task of making the path of *enough* the well-trodden one.

A friend who read a draft of this book challenged me to help readers decide on at least one practical thing they could do to tread that path. She also felt it was important that I offer suggestions that would not make people look silly, because so many of us worry about what other people will think if we do something countercultural. However, I really cannot be prescriptive and give a to-do list of non-silly things. My friend was not trying to be reductionist or simplistic; she was highlighting the need for people to receive suggestions about points at which they can enter the path of *enough*, or deepen their involvement. But each one of us must decide what steps to take. So do what you can, depending on where you are starting from. Respond in ways that seem right for the circumstances. But at the same time, be daring and if some *enough*-inspired action or way of being feels right to you, then risk the ridicule of others who may not understand it.

I don't know where the readers of this book are positioned on the path of *enough* or in the world. I only know that if you have got this far, you must be interested. You might be a designated local, national or world leader; perhaps you identify yourself as a citizen-leader, or maybe you are just now more concerned with personal issues. We all probably have something to add to our repertoire of *enough*-based responses to the world, and none of us is ever finished learning about *enough*. I also know that all of us need to attend to the public and the private dimensions of *enough*, because both individual and social transformation are essential.

The movement of *enough* encourages us to connect the personal and the political, as all good social movements do. From a beginning point in one's own life, one can connect personal issues to more abstract social and economic analysis at the level of the wider system. And one can also come to understand a great deal about the broader national and international contexts. And for those who are already activists in the public arena, it is crucial to also practice *enough* in private life. The personal, political, economic, social and cultural are all connected and we ignore any one of them at our peril.

Tasks for the daring

Your chief tasks with regard to *enough* are to develop your capacity to be philosophers and to cultivate hope. While these may not seem ultra-practical, they are essential, because hope and philosophy make up a strong foundation for any other steps you take.

If we make philosophy a living everyday practice and way of life, it becomes much more than an activity that academics do professionally and theoretically. Instead, we take the philosophical road that is constantly asking "how should we live?" Philosophy can help us develop a vision of a good and moral life, but with a focus on certain principles and attitudes, rather than the specific forms of such a life. Principles or attitudes can help us distinguish what is significant from what is trivial and can act as a guide when we have to make choices. A principled vision can also help us cope with the cynicism of others, or the self-consciousness we might feel when we act in countercultural ways.

It takes a bit of effort to cultivate hope, and it is easier to be despairing or cynical. Unfortunately, many people today find it easier to envisage the destruction of nature, ecosystems and biodiversity and the continuation of social injustice than to imagine that we could create a better world. To be hopeful requires commitment and courage, even though you do not know how the situation will turn out. You have to bear frustration but without becoming arrogant or bitter, and you have to believe that the good thing, the thing one wants, will come,[1] even though you do not know right now what that good thing may look like. So you also have to be steadfast, which is another characteristic of hope.

Concentrate on possibility: the best insurance for a decent future is *what we do now*; we can set the seeds for the future in our present actions. Whatever we choose to do, we have to get the balance right between being conscious of the future and understanding its relation to the present. On the one hand, we affect the future by our actions in the present. But on the other hand, we can be too obsessed with predicting the future accurately, in order to outwit it and insure ourselves against it. Moreover, trying to predict accurately is impossible, but we can become obsessed with it so much that it induces a paralysis: we do nothing because we cannot be certain how it will turn out. We can live in the present, learn from the past and plan for the future, but not invest too much in it.

The more we exercise our philosophical muscles, the more adept and capable we become as philosophers, and the more we deepen our innate human capacity to learn. We can all model a life of learning about *enough*. As we learn, more options open up to us, intellectually and imaginatively. We can keep the many-layered philosophy and practice of *enough* moving, living, changing, responding, questioning and self-examining.

Coping well in the present

It is always easier to cultivate hope and a sense of possibility, if one is coping well with present circumstances. You can use *enough* to create a platform of personal stability for yourself. Avoid being too busy, or having a surfeit of possessions; cut down on unnecessary decisions. It is true liberation to know how to live well with just the right amount of material accumulation. Our choices are limited only by our imaginations. It is very rewarding to develop financial intelligence, stay out of debt and keep money in its proper place in your life. Separating ourselves as much as possible from the need for money is a crucial part of freeing ourselves to cope within the system, to critique and resist it, and to create something new.

Maybe your entry point for coping is to develop your inner compass of *enough* with regard to eating, drinking, drug taking, gambling, shopping or some other compulsive activity. This would be different from finding self-control; it concerns finding enough self-knowledge to help yourself. Maybe you need to sort out other personal issues concerning busyness or addiction to work. If you are constantly struggling in your personal life with these kinds of issues, you are never going to find the time to participate in public efforts for change.

Or perhaps you need to get enough sleep, rest, time alone, silence, self-care, good food or comfort. It could be you need more time with the people you love, so that you can participate in and learn to value all the caring activities that exist in the invisible economy. Or maybe your challenge is learning to receive care and love. You could consider starting or joining a listening community. Another entry point might be learning to explore your own feelings, to be patient with yourself, to learn to appreciate modest things or to see the beauty in the ordinary.

Your entry point might be growing something in your garden, or in a pot if you have no garden. It could be learning to cook, to repair things, or to increase other practical skills. It might be market-oriented and might mean making a commitment to support local food preparers and growers.

Simple acts of coping, based on *enough*, are an implicit critique of the dominant culture of more. They also constitute resistance to that culture and the creation of something new. However, all four of these responses – coping, resisting, critiquing and creating – need to be taken into the public arena also. Your task of being hopeful will be easier if you see yourself as part of a whole, or of a connected movement. Social movements enhance actual possibility, because they support individual changes and transformations. The level of change required needs collective support and collective resistance and if these are absent, people can become despondent and feel powerless.

Join a conversation with others about these issues; talk to a family member or friend about some of the ideas in this book, whether you liked or hated them. If there was something you disliked, maybe you could go back and re-read it and think more about why you dislike it and how you might improve that idea or achieve its aim in a different way. Read some of the books mentioned here or visit some of the websites; take a relevant class or course, write a poem or paint something about *enough*; host a reading group, study circle or conversation café for this book or any others you read

Channel your knowledge into public movements that can create better ways to live. With gardening, transport, technology, recycling, cooking and growing, you can pass on what you know and learn from others. Join any of the existing movements like Slow Food, a local credit union, a local exchange system, swap club or transition-town group. Or join a group campaigning for carbon quotas or a Citizens' Income. You don't have to start a new organization; there is probably one out there that matches what you want to do. You can also bring your knowledge and your questions into groups to which you already belong, such as church, trade union, sports club, study group or workplace. With other people, do what you can to restore democratic public space such as meeting places, town squares and soap boxes, where people can speak, listen and learn about possibilities for change. The internet is an important kind of public space — and very democratic — but computer contact is no substitute for physical public civic space.

If you find you are having success with a local movement, you could go a bit further afield, into national civil society, international civil society, even into government. That is not to say that we should all try to get elected. It would be good of course if some movement people got into government. But it is also important to maintain civil society – all those grouping and activities that exist outside the state and the free-trade market — so that government is always reminded of its responsibilities. Politics often seems far removed from us or very abstract. But a thriving civil society is how people and government communicate. It links knowledge to action and makes politics something tangible and living.

Efforts for change are most successful when people work together and have a sense of connectedness. Solidarity can amplify the voice of the movement of *enough*; and when your voice has a better chance of being heard, your hope is maintained. The vision of hypercapitalism has been very coherent and therefore has been heard clearly. We need the worldview of *enough* to be equally clear, although that is not the same as being fixed or rigid. The worldview for the movement combines a quest for coherence, wholeness and connections, with fluidity and flexibility. The movement should have its own distinct flavor but must not be coercive.

Enough of this book

This book is a record of my path through *enough*; it does not show every detail of the terrain I covered and all I have seen. I wanted to tell you everything but of course that would have made for a very unwieldy book. Part of me also wanted the book to be perfect, to get across to you in a successful way all the possibilities that are open to us at this time. Writing takes things apart, and is thus fairly inadequate when it comes to demonstrating connections. At times during the process, I despaired of my attempts. I kept going because I believe that writing, when people read it, becomes an important means of keeping ideas and knowledge living and dynamic. So to get the ideas out there, I had to let go of my desire for perfection. After all, *enough* is about being fully human, with all of the attendant imperfections. I had to put *enough* into practice and limit both the content and my desire for perfection and, in the end, I offer a work that expresses my own hope, however imperfectly.

Take these ideas and craft your own story of possibility from them. On the journey, stay connected with others who are exploring *enough* also. I have tried to present certain ideas and their meanings and to ask related questions. You may perceive other meanings and pose different questions. But we need to accompany each other on the road, not act as competitors in this endeavour. For all of us who take this path, there will be moments of despair and moments when our hope is renewed. We will find ourselves walking with unlikely companions. And we will always need to work to integrate our experience and insights into our daily lives.

The image of the journey has its limitations, for our usual response to the idea of a journey is to see it as having a fixed end point. But with *enough*, we can probably never say, "I have arrived". There is always the unexpected, which challenges us in ways we might not be able to anticipate from where we are now. The important thing is that we respond in some way, drawing on our visions and on the principles of *enough*.

If you would like to let me know about your adventures on the path of *enough*, I would be delighted to hear from you. You can contact me through the website for this book, www.enoughisplenty.net, or you can write to me:

Anne B Ryan
c/o Department of Adult and Community Education
NUI Maynooth
Maynooth
Co Kildare, Ireland.

NOTES TO CHAPTER 1

[1] Dawson, Jonathan (2006) *Ecovillages: New Frontiers for Sustainability.* Schumacher Briefings no 7. Totnes, Devon: Green Books.

[2] You can read accounts of lifestyles like these in books like Dominguez, Joe and Robin, Vicki (1999, first published 1992) *Your Money or Your Life.* Harmondsworth: Penguin; Ryan, Anne B (2002) *Balancing Your Life.* Dublin: The Liffey Press. See also websites such as *Transition Cultures* www.transitioncultures.org and *Simple Living Network* www.simpleliving.net.

[3] But see Le Guin, Ursula K (1988) *Always Coming Home.* London: Grafton; Blumenfeld, Yorick (1999) *2099: A Eutopia: Prospects for Tomorrow.* London: Thames and Hudson.

[4] See www.resurgence.org

[5] McKibben, Bill (2004) *Enough: Genetic Engineering and Human Nature.* London: Bloomsbury, page 227.

[6] Le Guin, Ursula K (2003) "Life in the Wider Household of Being", an interview with Ursula K le Guin by Erika Milo for *North by Northwest*, Nov. www.northbynorthwest.org

[7] O'Sullivan, Edmund V (1999) *Transformative learning: Educational vision for the 21st century.* Toronto: University of Toronto Press, page 231.

[8] McKibben, Bill (2004) *Enough: Genetic Engineering and Human Nature.* London: Bloomsbury, page 214.

[9] Brandt, Barbara (1995) *Whole Life Economics: Revaluing Daily Life.* Philadelphia, PA and Gabriola Island, BC: New Society Publishers.

[10] McKibben, Bill (2004) *Enough: Genetic Engineering and Human Nature.* London: Bloomsbury, page 217.

[11] McKibben, Bill (2004) *Enough: Genetic Engineering and Human Nature.* London: Bloomsbury, page 218.

[12] Tudge, Colin (2004) *So Shall We Reap: What's gone wrong with the world's food – and how to fix it.* London: Penguin.

[13] Eagleton, Terry (2003) *After Theory*. Cambridge, MA: Basic Books.

[14] Gottlieb, Roger S. (2003) *A Spirituality of Resistance: Finding a Peaceful Heart and Protecting the Earth*. Lanham, Maryland: Rowman and Littlefield, page 32.

[15] Gottlieb, Roger S. (2003) *A Spirituality of Resistance: Finding a Peaceful Heart and Protecting the Earth*. Lanham, Maryland: Rowman and Littlefield.

[16] Gottlieb, Roger S. (2003) *A Spirituality of Resistance: Finding a Peaceful Heart and Protecting the Earth*. Lanham, Maryland: Rowman and Littlefield, pages 13-18.

[17] Selby, David (2002) "The signature of the Whole: Radical Interconnectedness and its Implications for Global and Environmental Education", pages 87- 88 in O'Sullivan, Edmund V., Amish Morell and Mary Ann O'Connor (eds), *Expanding the Boundaries of Transformative Learning*. New York: Palgrave Macmillan, pages 77 – 93.

[18] Goodman, Anne (2003) *Now What? Developing our Future: Understanding our Place in the Unfolding Universe*. New York: Peter Lang, page 170.

[19] Sheldrake, Rupert (1991) *The Rebirth of Science and Nature: The Greening of Science and God*. New York: Bantam, page 95. Cited in Goodman, Anne (2003) *Now What? Developing our Future: Understanding our Place in the Unfolding Universe*. New York: Peter Lang, page 169.

[20] O'Sullivan, Edmund V. and Taylor, Marilyn M. (2004) "Glimpses of an Ecological Consciousness", in Edmund O'Sullivan and Marilyn Taylor (eds) *Learning Toward an Ecological Consciousness*. New York: Palgrave Macmillan, page 21.

[21] Anne Goodman notes that the theme of "survive, critique and create" originates with Thomas Berry, and is developed in Brian Swimme, Thomas Berry and Edmund O'Sullivan. I have added resistance, following Roger Gottlieb.

See Goodman, Anne (2003) *Now What? Developing our Future: Understanding our Place in the Unfolding Universe*. New York: Peter Lang, pages 163-7;

Gottlieb, Roger S. (2003) *A Spirituality of Resistance: Finding a Peaceful Heart and Protecting the Earth*. Lanham, Maryland: Rowman and Littlefield.;

Swimme, Brian and Berry, Thomas (1992) *The Universe Story: An Autobiography from Planet Earth*. San Francisco: Harper and Row;

O'Sullivan, Edmund V (1999) *Transformative learning: Educational vision for the 21st century*. Toronto: University of Toronto Press.

22 Goodman, Anne (2003) *Now What? Developing our Future: Understanding our Place in the Unfolding Universe*. New York: Peter Lang, page 167ff.

23 Miles, Angela (2002) "Feminist Perspectives on globalization and Integrative and Transformative Learning", page 23 in O'Sullivan, Edmund V., Amish Morell and Mary Ann O'Connor (eds) *Expanding the Boundaries of Transformative Learning*. New York: Palgrave Macmillan: 23-34.

24 Gablik, Suzi (2002) *Living the Magical Life: An oracular adventure*. Grand Rapids, MI: Phanes Press, page 206.

25 Gablik, Suzi (2002) *Living the Magical Life: An oracular adventure*. Grand Rapids, MI: Phanes Press, page 110.

26 Futurism is rooted in modernist thinking. See Goodman, Anne (2003) *Now What? Developing our Future: Understanding our Place in the Unfolding Universe*. New York: Peter Lang, pages 201-3.

27 Princen, Thomas, Maniates, Michael and Conca, Ken (2002) "Confronting Consumption". Introduction to Princen, Thomas, Maniates, Michael and Conca, Ken (eds) *Confronting Consumption*. Cambridge MA and London: The MIT Press, page 14. See also George, Susan (2004) *Another world is possible if ...* London: Verso.

[28] Distinctions made in Goodman, Anne (2003) *Now What? Developing our Future: Understanding our Place in the Unfolding Universe*. New York: Peter Lang, pages 303-4.

NOTES TO CHAPTER 2

[1] Mumford, Lewis (1944) *The Condition of Man*. New York: Harcourt, Brace. Cited in Goodman, Anne (2003) *Now What? Developing our Future: Understanding our Place in the Unfolding Universe*. New York: Peter Lang, page 47.

[2] McKibben, Bill (2004) *Enough: Genetic Engineering and Human Nature*. London: Bloomsbury, page 203.

[3] Tudge, Colin (2004) *So Shall We Reap: What's gone wrong with the world's food – and how to fix it*. London: Penguin, page 303.

[4] David C. Korten, *Globalizing Civil Socity* (sic), at www.davidkorten.org/globalizing_civil_society. Accessed August 22nd, 2008. Originally written as a report to the United Nations Conference on Human Settlement, 1997.

[5] Hopton, Ian "Work, gift and theft", *Resurgence* 235, page 21.

[6] Tudge, Colin (2004) *So Shall We Reap: What's gone wrong with the world's food – and how to fix it*. London: Penguin, page 382

[7] Reece, Erik (2006) "Moving Mountains: The battle for justice comes to the coal fields of Appalachia". *Orion* www.orion.org

[8] Korten, David C. (1999) *The Post-Corporate World: Life After Capitalism*. San Francisco: Berrett Koehler and West Hartford: Kumarian Press.

[9] Foot, Paul (2006) *The Vote: How It Was Won and How It Was Undermined*. London: Penguin.

[10] Tudge, Colin (2004) So Shall We Reap: What's gone wrong with the world's food – and how to fix it. London: Penguin, page 280.

[11] Princen, Thomas, Maniates, Michael and Conca, Ken (2002) "Conclusion: to Confront Consumption", in Princen, Thomas, Maniates, Michael and Conca, Ken (2002) (eds) *Confronting Consumption*. Cambridge MA and London: The MIT Press,

pages 317-328.

[12] For more on this, see Levett, Roger, with Ian Christie, Michael Jacobs and Riki Therivel (2003) *A Better Choice of Choice: Quality of life, consumption and economic growth.* London: Fabian Society, page 40.

[13] Lucas, Caroline and Shiva, Vandana (2005) "G8's free trade project is here to stay –along with world poverty". *The Guardian*, July 4th.

[14] Shiva, Vandana (2005) "Two myths that keep the world poor". *The Ecologist.* July-August.

[15] Tudge, Colin (2004) *So Shall We Reap: What's gone wrong with the world's food – and how to fix it.* London: Penguin, page 385.

[16] Spretnak, Charlene (1999) *The Resurgence of the Real.* New York: Routledge.

[17] Shiva, Vandana (2005) "Flat vision". Review of Thomas Friedman (2005) *The World is Flat.* London: Allen Lane. In *Resurgence* 232, pages 60-61.

[18] George, Susan (2003, second edition) *The Lugano Report: On Preserving Capitalism in the Twenty-First Century.* London: Pluto Press.

[19] George, Susan (2004) *Another world is possible if …* London: Verso. Page x

[20] Gottlieb, Roger S. (2003) A Spirituality of Resistance: Finding a Peaceful Heart and Protecting the Earth. Lanham, Maryland: Rowman and Littlefield, page 65.

[21] Bunting, Madeleine (2004). *Willing Slaves: How the Overwork Culture is Ruining our Lives.* London: Harper Collins.

[22] Milani, Brian (1998) *Beyond Globalization: The Struggle to Redefine Wealth.* www.greeneconomics.net?MAI.htm, accessed 23 Feb 2004, page 6.

[23] Hochschild, Arlie Russell (2003) *The commercialization of intimate life: notes from home and work.* Berkeley: University of California Press.

[24] Abbott, Chris, Rogers, Paul and Sloboda, John (2006) *Global*

Responses to Global Threats: Sustainable security for the 21ˢᵗ Century. Oxford: Oxford Research Group. www.oxfordresearchgroup.org.uk

25 McKibben, Bill (2004) *Enough: Genetic Engineering and Human Nature*. London: Bloomsbury

26 Krastev, Ivan (2006) "The energy route to Russian democracy", *Open Democracy*. www.opendemocracy.net

NOTES TO CHAPTER 3

1 Lloyd, Christopher (2006) "Reforming the Common Agricultural Policy", in *Resurgence* 234, page 6.

2 Crowley, Ethel (2006) *Land Matters: Power struggles in rural Ireland*. Dublin: Lilliput, page 15.

3 Lloyd, Christopher (2006) "Reforming the Common Agricultural Policy", in *Resurgence* 234, pages 6,7.

4 Pollan, Michael (2006) *The Omnivore's Dilemma: A Natural History of Four Meals*. New York: Penguin, page 50.

5 Tudge, Colin (2007) "Enlightened Agriculture", in *Resurgence* 242, page 31.

6 Tudge, Colin (2004) *So Shall We Reap: What's gone wrong with the world's food – and how to fix it*. London: Penguin, page 22.

7 Maynard, Robin and Shiva, Vandana (2008) "Feeding People or Cars?" *Resurgence* 247, page 19.

8 Tudge, Colin (2007) *Feeding People is Easy*. Pari: Paripublishing, pages 123-4.

9 Humane Farming Association Slaughter Campaign. www.hfa.org/campaigns/slaughter.html. Accessed 25 Sept 2007.

10 Some traditional diets did rely heavily on meat and other animal products such as eggs, cheese and milk, especially in places where it was easier to raise animals than to grow plant food. These kinds of traditional diets also provided a good balance of nutrients since the animals had a natural diet.

11 Lawrence, Felicity, (2006) "Britain's fertility crisis". *Guardian*

Review, page 10.

[12] Fallon, Sally (2001) *Nourishing Traditions*. Washington: New Trends Publishing.

Pollan, Michael (2006) *The Omnivore's Dilemma: A Natural History of Four Meals*. New York: Penguin, pages 268-9.

[13] Hanley, Jesse, Lee, John R and Hopkins, Virginia (2005) *What Your Doctor May Not Tell You About Premenopause: Balancing your hormones and your life from thirty to fifty*. New York: Warner Wellness, page 305.

[14] We are also exposed to xenoestrogens in tapwater, through the plastics used to wrap and store food and water, through atmospheric pollution and through various petrol-based creams and lotions we use.

[15] Bellarby, Jessica, Foereid, Bente, Hastings, Astley and Smith, Pete (2008) *Cool Farming: Climate impacts of agriculture and mitigation potential*. Amsterdam: Greenpeace International (Authors from the school of Biological Sciences, University of Aberdeen).

[16] Crowley, Ethel (2006) *Land Matters: Power struggles in rural Ireland*. Dublin: Lilliput, pages 82-7.

[17] Lloyd, Christopher (2006) "Reforming the Common Agricultural Policy", in *Resurgence* 234, page 7.

[18] Tudge, Colin (2007) *Feeding People is Easy*. Pari: Paripublishing, page 136.

[19] Maynard, Robin and Shiva, Vandan (2008) "Feeding People or Cars?" *Resurgence* 247, pages 18-19.

[20] Tudge, Colin (2004) *So Shall We Reap: What's gone wrong with the world's food – and how to fix it*. London: Penguin, page 310.

[21] Shiva, Vandana (2007) "Food freedom", *Resurgence* 242, page 24.

[22] Siegle, Lucy (2005) "Ethical Living". *Observer Magazine*, 26 June.

[23] Cocker, Mark (2006) "Magpies of the landscape", in *Guardian Review*, June 24th. Review of Sue Clifford and Angela King

(2006) *England in Particular: a celebration of the commonplace, the local, the vernacular and the distinctive*. London: Hodder and Stoughton.

34 Tudge, Colin (2004) *So Shall We Reap: What's gone wrong with the world's food – and how to fix it*. London: Penguin, page 374.

25 You can read more about this in Pollan, Michael (2006) *The Omnivore's Dilemma: A Natural History of Four Meals*. New York: Penguin. See also Shiva, Vandana (2007) "Food freedom", *Resurgence* 242, pages 22-24

Cargill, ADM and Monsanto are the dominant companies.

NOTES TO CHAPTER 4

1 For example, Brandt, Barbara (1995) *Whole Life Economics: Revaluing Daily Life*. Philadelphia, PA and Gabriola Island, BC: New Society Publishers.

Douthwaite, Richard (2000, second edition) *The Growth Illusion: How Economic Growth has Enriched the Few, Impoverished the many, and Endangered the Planet*. Dublin: The Lilliput Press, in association with New Society Publishers and Green Books.

2 Meyer, Aubrey (2005) *Contraction and Convergence*: The Global Solution to Climate Change. Schumacher Briefing no 5. Totnes. Devon: Green Books.

Hillman, Mayer, with Tina Fawcett (2004). *How We Can Save the Planet*. London: Penguin.

3 *The Guardian Weekend*, January 5th, 2008, page 31.

4 Wright, Martin (2005) "Diminuendo", interview with Aubrey Meyer, originator of Contraction and Convergence framework, in Green Futures www.greenfutures.org. Wright cites as supporters Michael Meacher, former British environment minister and Adair Turner, ex-head of Confederation of British Industry, now with Merrill Lynch.

5 At the November 2000 negotiations on Kyoto in The Hague. See James Bruges, review of the first edition of Meyer, Aubrey

(1999) *Contraction and Convergence: The Global Solution to Chinate Change.* Schumacher Briefing no 5. Totnes. Devon: Green Books. www.gci.org.uk/ccbook.html#7.

6   Retallack, Simon (2006) "Climate Change: the global test". *Open Democracy*, Nov 10th. www.opendemocracy.net

7   Hillman, Mayer (2005) "Living beyond the planet's limits". *Open Democracy*, www.opendemocracy.net

8   Retallack, Simon 2006 "Climate Change: the global test". Open Democracy, Nov 10 www.opendemocracy.net

9   International Panel on Climate Change, 2007

10 Mayer Hillman says we need to reduce to 1.5 tons each, George Monbiot says we need to reduce to 0.8 tons. The main point is that it is a big reduction for those currently emitting over 10 tons. The Cap and Share campaign estimates that in the first year of a scheme, each adult would be able to emit just under 4 tons, with reductions in subsequent years. Currently, well-off people in Edinburgh emit 6.79 tons on transport. Clearly, transport would be one of the sectors most affected.
    Hillman, Mayer(2005) "Living beyond the planet's limits". *Open Democracy*, www.opendemocracy.net;
    Monbiot, George (2006). *Heat: How to Stop the Planet Burning.* London: Allen Lane. www.capandshare.org; www.climateco-operation.org/cap_and_share

11 see The Global Commons Institute at www.gci.org.uk

12 Karpf, Anne (2002) "A chain reaction", in *Guardian Weekend*, Nov 2nd.

13 Karpf, Anne (2002) "A chain reaction", in *Guardian Weekend*. Nov 2nd.

14 Monbiot, George (2006) *Heat: How to Stop the Planet Burning.* London: Allen Lane, pages 190-98.

15 Roberts, Ian and Hillman, Mayer (2006) "Roads to ruin", in *Resurgence Magazine* No 235, page 16.

16 John Jopling (2006), letter to *The Kerryman*, June. Monbiot, George (2006) *Heat: How to Stop the Planet Burning.* London:

Allen Lane, page 46.

[17] Douthwaite. Richard (2007) "Cap and Share", in *Resurgence Magazine* No 240, January-February, page 24.

[18] Douthwaite, Richard (2007) "Cap and Share", in *Resurgence Magazine* No 240, January-February, page 24.

[19] Susan George makes a similar point with regard to land registration. George, Susan (2004) *Another world is possible if...* London: Verso, pages 151-2.

[20] www.grameen-info.org
Kahn, Farida (2006) "Muhammed Yunus: an economics for peace", *Open Democracy*, www.opendemocracy.net

[21] Richard Douthwaite uses the term "EBCUs" (emissions-backed currency units), see Douthwaite, Richard (1999) *The Ecology of Money*. Schumacher Briefings no 4. Totnes, Devon: Green Books.
George Monbiot suggests "icecaps", in Monbiot, George (2006) *Heat: How to Stop the Planet Burning*. London: Allen Lane.

[22] Roberts, Ian and Hillman, Mayer (2006) "Roads to ruin", in *Resurgence Magazine* No 215, page 16.

[23] Milani, Brian (1998) *Beyond Globalization: The Struggle to Redefine Wealth*. www.greeneconomics.net?MAI.htm, page 9, accessed 23 Feb,2004.

[24] Stiglitz, Joseph (2006) in *The Miami Herald*, November 15.

[25] Hillman, Mayer, with Tina Fawcett (2004). *How We Can Save the Planet*. London: Penguin, pages 3-4.

[26] Hillman, Mayer, with Tina Fawcett (2004). *How We Can Save the Planet*. London: Penguin, pages 133-4.

[27] Hillman, Mayer, with Tina Fawcett (2004). *How We Can Save the Planet*. London: Penguin, pages 133-4.

[28] Douthwaite, Richard (2007) "Cap and Share", in *Resurgence Magazine* No 240.

[29] Levett, Roger, with Ian Christie, Michael Jacobs and Riki Therivel (2003) *A Better Choice of Choice: Quality of life,*

consumption and economic growth. London: Fabian Society.

30 World Health Organization, cited in *You and Yours*, BBC Radio 4, 27 Oct, 2005.

31 Hemenway, Toby (2001) *Gaia's Garden: A Guide to Home-Scale Permaculture*. Vermont: Chelsea Green Publishing Company, pages 26-9.

32 In 2005, global anti-poverty campaigners came together under the banner of "Make Poverty History", attracting unprecedented numbers of demonstrators, especially at a meeting of the G8 in Edinburgh. See www.makepovertyhistory.org

33 Wright, Martin (2005) "Diminuendo", interview with Aubrey Meyer, originator of Contraction and Convergence framework, in *Green Futures*. www.greenfutures.org.

34 Monbiot, George (2006) *Heat: How to Stop the Planet Burning*. London: Allen Lane, page 73 ff.

35 Abbott, Chris, Rogers, Paul and Sloboda, John (2006) *Global Responses to Global Threats: Sustainable security for the 21st Century*. Oxford: Oxford Research Group.

36 Monbiot, George (2006) *Heat: How to Stop the Planet Burning*. London: Allen Lane, page xv.

37 Joseph Stiglitz argues that globalization needs to be made more democratic and that already existing organizations like the WTO could be harnessed to do so; however, he does not mention carbon trading. See Stiglitz, Joseph E (2006) *Making Globalisation Work*. London and New York: Penguin.

38 Van Parijs, Philippe (2000) "Response" in *Boston Review*, bostonreview.net/BR2S.5/vanparijs2.htnil. page 2, accessed Nov 6, 2006.

39 Van Parijs, Philippe (2000) "Response" in *Boston Review*, bostonreview.net/BR2S.5/vanparijs2.htnil. page 2, accessed Nov 6, 2006.

40 See www.capandshare.org. The model has been developed by the NGOs Feasta and the New Economics Foundation.

41 Paul Rogers makes similar points: "Climate change: threat and

promise", in *Open Democracy*, Nov 2006.
www.opendemocracy.net

42 www.capandshare.org

NOTES TO CHAPTER 5

1 Lord, Clive (2003) *A Citizens' Income: a foundation for a sustainable world.* Charlbury: Jon Carpenter. Page 69.

2 Department of the Taoiseach, *White Paper on Basic Income*, Dublin, 2002 www.taoiseach.gov.ie.
Conference of Religious in Ireland
www.cori.ie/justice/basic_income/index.htm.

3 Lord, Clive (2003) *A Citizens' Income: a foundation for a sustainable world.* Charlbury: Jon Carpenter.
Van Parijs, Philippe (1997) "The Need for Basic Income: An Interview with Philippe Van Parijs by Christopher Bertram". *Imprints.* www.eis.bris.ac.uk/~plcdib/imprints.vanparijsinterview.html. Accessed 6 Nov 2006

4 Andrews, Cecile (2006) *Slow is Beautiful: new visions of community, leisure and joie de vivre.* Gabriola Island, BC: New Society Publishers.
Schor, Juliet (1998) *The Overspent American.* New York: Basic Books.

5 See Princen, Thomas, Maniates, Michael and Conca, Ken (2002) (eds) *Confronting Consumption.* Cambridge MA and London: The MIT Press.

6 Lord, Clive (2003) *A Citizens' Income: a foundation for a sustainable world.* Charlbury: Jon Carpenter. Page 97.

7 Van Parijs, Philippe (1997) "The Need for Basic Income: An Interview with Philippe Van Parijs by Christopher Bertram". *Imprints,* page 4. www.eis.bris.ac.uk/~plcdib/imprints.vanparijsinterview.html. Accessed 6 Nov 2006

8 Lord, Clive (2003) *A Citizens' Income: a foundation for a sustainable world.* Charlbury: Jon Carpenter. Page 89.

9 Blythman, Joanna (2005) *Shopped: The Shocking Power of British*

Supermarkets. London: Fourth Estate.

[10] Tudge, Colin (2004) *So Shall We Reap: What's gone wrong with the world's food – and how to fix it.* London: Penguin.

[11] Lord, Clive (2003) *A Citizens' Income: a foundation for a sustainable world.* Charlbury: Jon Carpenter. Page 73.

[12] Glyn, Andrew (2006) *Capitalism Unleashed: Finance, Globalization and Welfare.* New York: Oxford University Press. Page 181.

[13] Lord, Clive (2003) *A Citizens' Income: a foundation for a sustainable world.* Charlbury: Jon Carpenter. Page 60.

[14] This is a central premise of Clive Lord's work. Lord, Clive (2003) *A Citizens' Income: a foundation for a sustainable world.* Charlbury: Jon Carpenter.

[15] *Citizens' Income Newsletter,* Issue One, 2007.

[16] Glyn, Andrew (2006) *Capitalism Unleashed: Finance, Globalization and Welfare.* New York: Oxford University Press. Page 181.

[17] Glyn, Andrew (2006) *Capitalism Unleashed: Finance, Globalization and Welfare.* New York: Oxford University Press. Page 180.

[18] Lord, Clive (2003) *A Citizens' Income: a foundation for a sustainable world.* Charlbury: Jon Carpenter. Page 65.

[19] Lord, Clive (2003) *A Citizens' Income: a foundation .for a sustainable world.* Charlbury: Jon Carpenter. Page 58.

[20] George, Susan (2004) *Another world is possible if ...* London: Verso, page 137.

[21] New Economics Foundation (NEF), "The price of power," 2004, www.neweconomics.org

[22] For example, George, Susan (2004) *Another world is possible if ...* London: Verso, page 138

[23] Joseph Stiglitz makes similar points about the WTO, although not in the context of a Citizens' Income. Stiglitz, Joseph E (2006) *Making Globalization Work.* London and New York: Penguin.

[24] Seager, Ashley (2007) "A land tax is 200 years overdue". *The Guardian*, January 8th. www.guardian.co.uk

[25] http://www.progress.org/geonomy/geonom153.htm;

[26] http://www.progress.org/geonomy/geonom153.htm

[27] Van Parijs, Philippe (1997) "The Need for Basic Income: An Interview with Philippe Van Parijs by Christopher Bertram". *Imprints*. Page 1. www.eis.bris.ac.uk/~plcdib/imprints.vanparijsinterview.html. Accessed 6 Nov 2006.
See also Schutz, Robert (1996) *The $30,000 Solution*. Santa Barbara, CA: Fithian Press.

[28] Lord, Clive (2003) *A Citizens' Income: a foundation for a sustainable world*. Charlbury: Jon Carpenter.

[29] Levett, Roger, with Ian Christie, Michael Jacobs and Riki Therivel (2003) *A Better Choice of Choice: Quality of life, consumption and economic growth*. London: Fabian Society, page 68.

[30] Pateman, Carole (2004) "Democratising Citizenship: Some Advantages of a Basic Income", in *Politics and Society* 32 (1): 89-105.
Van Parijs, Philippe (2001) *What's Wrong with a Free Lunch?* Boston: Beacon Press.

[31] Van Parijs, Philippe (1997) "The Need for Basic Income: An Interview with Philippe Van Parijs by Christopher Bertram". *Imprints*. Page 7. www.eis.bris.ac.uk/~plcdib/imprints.vanparijsinterview.html. Accessed 6 Nov 2006.

[32] Glyn, Andrew (2006) *Capitalism Unleashed: Finance, Globalization and Welfare*. New York: Oxford University Press. Page 182.

[33] Levett, Roger, with Ian Christie, Michael Jacobs and Riki Therivel (2003) *A Better Choice of Choice: Quality of life, consumption and economic growth*. London: Fabian Society. page 66.

[34] Levitas, Ruth (1998) *The Inclusive Society? Social Exclusion and New Labour*. London: Macmillan

[35] Not just people are citizens of the globe; all living things could be regarded as citizens. But since they don't need an income, I confine the discussion here to people.

[36] Glyn, Andrew (2006) *Capitalism Unleashed: Finance, Globalization and Welfare*. New York: Oxford University Press, page 183.

[37] See numerous publications by the Oxford Research Group, www.oxfordresearchgroup.org.
"Wild Arabia: The Natural History of the Middle East2, BBC Radio 4, Aug 27th, 2007.

[38] George, Susan (2004) *Another world is possible if ...* London: Verso. Page151.

[39] Convention on Biological Diversity, cited in Harding, Stephan (2006) *Animate Earth: Science, Intuition and Gaia*. Totnes: Green Books page 228.

[40] Bambrick, Laura (2006) "Wollstonecraft's Dilemma: Is a Citizen's Income the Answer?", in *Citizen's Income Newsletter* Issue 2, page 6. www.citizensincome.org

[41] Glyn, Andrew (2006) *Capitalism Unleashed: Finance, Globalization and Welfare*. New York: Oxford University Press, pages 182-3.

[42] Lord, Clive (2003) *A Citizens' Income: a foundation for a sustainable world*. Charlbury: Jon Carpenter, page 73.

[43] Dominguez, Joe and Robin, Vicki (1997, second edition) *Your Money or Your Life: Transforming Your Relationship with Money and Achieving Financial Independence*. Harmondsworth: Penguin.
Ryan, Anne B. (2002) *Balancing Your Life: A Practical Guide to Work, Time, Money and Happiness*. Dublin: The Liffey Press.
The Simple Living Foundation www.simpleliving.net.
Swenson, Richard A. (1998) *The Overload Syndrome: Learning to Live within Your Limits*. Colorado Springs: Navpress.

[44] Lange, Elizabeth A. (2004) "Transformative and Restorative Learning: A Vital Dialectic for Sustainable Societies", in *Adult*

Education Quarterly 54 (2): 121-139, pages 127-9.

45 Levett, Roger, with Ian Christie, Michael Jacobs and Riki Therivel (2003) *A Better Choice of Choice: Quality of life, consumption and economic growth.* London: Fabian Society.

46 Lord, Clive (2003) *A Citizens' Income: a foundation for a sustainable world.* Charlbury: Jon Carpenter. Page 73.

47 Brandt, Barbara (1995) *Whole Life Economics: Revaluing Daily Life.* Philadelphia, PA and Gabriola Island, BC: New Society Publishers. page 201.

48 Brandt, Barbara (1995) *Whole Life Economics: Revaluing Daily Life.* Philadelphia, PA and Gabriola Island, BC: New Society Publishers. page 201.

49 Brandt, Barbara (1995) *Whole Life Economics: Revaluing Daily Life.* Philadelphia, PA and Gabriola Island, BC: New Society Publishers. page 201.

50 Van Parijs, Philippe (1997) "The Need for Basic Income: An Interview with Philippe Van Parijs by Christopher Bertram". *Imprints.* Page 9. www.eis.bris.ac.uk/~plcdib/imprints.vanparijsinterview.html. Accessed 6 Nov 2006.

51 Lord, Clive (2003) *A Citizens' Income: a foundation for a sustainable world.* Charlbury: Jon Carpenter. Page 55.

52 Lord, Clive (2003) *A Citizens' Income: a foundation for a sustainable world.* Charlbury: Jon Carpenter. Page 113.

53 Additional sources of information:
Citizen's Income Newsletter www.citizensincome.org;
Robertson, James (1998) *Beyond the Dependency Culture: People, Power and Responsibility.* Adamantine Press. (Now out of print, but available to download from www.jamesrobertson.com.)
The Basic Income European Network, www.etes.ucl.ac.be/BIEN/Sitemap.htm.
Conference of Religious in Ireland www.cori.ie/justice/SharingLimitedResources_03.htm.

South African New Economics (SANE) Foundation, www.sane.org

54 Dominguez, Joe and Robin, Vicki (1997, second edition) *Your Money or Your Life: Transforming Your Relationship with Money and Achieving Financial Independence*. Harmondsworth: Penguin.

Naish, John (2008) *Enough: Breaking free from the world of more*. London: Hodder and Stoughton.

Ryan, Anne B (2002) *Balancing Your Life: A Practical Guide to Work, Time, Money and Happiness*. Dublin: The Liffey Press.

The Simple Living Foundation www.simpleliving.net

Swenson, Richard A. (1998) *The Overload Syndrome: Learning to Live Within Your Limits*. Colorado Springs: Navpress.

Schwarz, Barry (2004) *The Paradox of Choice: Why More Is Less*. New York: Harper Collins.

NOTES TO CHAPTER 6

1 Tudge, Colin (2004) *So Shall We Reap: What's gone wrong with the world's food – and how to fix it*. London: Penguin, pages 270-1.

2 Colin Tudge uses the terms "Enlightened Agriculture" and "craft-level farming", see Tudge, Colin (2004) *So Shall We Reap: What's gone wrong with the world's food – and how to fix it*. London: Penguin, and (2007) *Feeding People is Easy*. Pari: Paripublishing. Jules Pretty uses the term "ecological agriculture", in Pretty, Jules (2002) *Agri-Culture: Reconnecting people, land and nature*. London: Earthscan and (2007) 'A Living From the Land', in *Resurgence*, 224: 27.

   "Local farming" is the term used by the International Society for Ecology and Culture (ISEC), see www.isec.org.uk

3 For a survey of 208 projects worldwide, see Pretty, Jules (2002) *Agri-Culture: Reconnecting people, land and nature*. London: Earthscan.

4 Tudge, Colin (2004) *So Shall We Reap: What's gone wrong with*

the world's food – and how to fix it. London: Penguin.

5 Hemenway, Toby (2001) *Gaia's Garden: A Guide to Home-Scale Permaculture*. Vermont: Chelsea Green Publishing Company.

6 Nielsen, Andrew (2007) *Cattle & The Environment, One Farmer's Perspective*. www.simpleliving.net, accessed 5 March 2007;

Pollan, Michael (2006) *The Omnivore's Dilemma: A Natural History of Four Meals*. New York: Penguin.

7 Tudge, Colin (2005) "Time for a peasant revolution", in *Resurgence* 230, page 15.

8 Lloyd, Christopher (2006) "Reforming the Common Agricultural Policy", in *Resurgence* 234, pages 6-8.

9 Whitefield, Patrick (2000, third edition) *How To Make A Forest Garden*. Hampshire: Permanent Publications, page 3.

10 Berry, Wendell (2001) "The Idea of a Local Economy". *Orion Magazine*, Winter.
http://www.oriononline.org/pages/om/archive_om/Berry/Local_ Economy.html

11 Tudge, Colin (2007) *Feeding People is Easy*. Pari: Paripublishing, pages 136-7.

12 Lloyd, Christopher (2006) "Reforming the Common Agricultural Policy", in *Resurgence* 234, pages 6-8.

13 Lloyd, Christopher (2006) "Reforming the Common Agricultural Policy", in *Resurgence* 234, page 8.

14 Lloyd, Christopher (2006) "Reforming the Common Agricultural Policy", in *Resurgence* 234, page 8.

15 See www.slowfood.com

16 Petrini, Carlo and Waters, Alice (2007) *Slow Food Nation*. New York: Random House.

17 "Our Food, Our Future", BBC Radio 4, 11 August 2008.

18 You can read more in Tudge, Colin (2004) *So Shall We Reap: What's gone wrong with the world's food – and how to fix it*. London: Penguin.

Tudge, Colin (2007) *Feeding People is Easy*. Pari:

Paripublishing.

See also www.colintudge.com

[19] Pollan, Michael (2006) *The Omnivore's Dilemma: A Natural History of Four Meals*. New York: Penguin, pages 240, 244.

[20] Pollan, Michael (2006) *The Omnivore's Dilemma: A Natural History of Four Meals*. New York: Penguin, page 254.

[21] On markets in benign capitalism see Tudge, Colin (2007) *Feeding People is Easy*. Pari: Paripublishing, pages 148-150.

On mindful markets see Korten, David (1998) *The Post-Corporate World: Life after capitalism*. West Hartford, CT: Kumarian Press.

[22] Pollan, Michael (2006) *The Omnivore's Dilemma: A Natural History of Four Meals*. New York: Penguin, page 254.

[23] Petrini, Carlo (2006) "The New Gastronomy". *Resurgence*, 236: 17.

[24] See www.unsig.it

[25] The Rodale Institute "Mitigating climate change with organic agriculture". www.rodaleinstitute.org/node/423

[26] Tudge, Colin (2007) *Feeding People is Easy*. Pari: Paripublishing, pages 146 and 173.

[27] Hemenway, Toby (2001) *Gaia's Garden: A Guide to Home-Scale Permaculture*. Vermont: Chelsea Green Publishing Company.

NOTES TO CHAPTER 7

[1] McIntosh, Alastair (2001) *Soil and Soul: People versus Corporate Power*. London: Aurum Press, page 28.

[2] Tudge, Colin (2004) *So Shall We Reap: What's gone wrong with the world's food – and how to fix it*. London: Penguin, page 358.

[3] Levett, Roger, with Ian Christie, Michael Jacobs and Riki Therivel (2003) *A Better Choice of Choice: Quality of life, consumption and economic growth*. London: Fabian Society, page 19.

[4] Wheatley, Margaret (2006) *Leadership and the New Science: Discovering Order in a Chaotic World*. San Francisco: Berrett-

Koehler Publications, page 46.

5   Dawson, Jonathan (2006) *Ecovillages: New Frontiers for Sustainability*. Schumacher Briefings no 7. Totnes, Devon: Green Books.

6   Maniates, Michael (2002) "Individualization: Plant a Tree, Buy a Bike, Save the World?" in Princen, Thomas, Maniates, Michael and Conca, Ken (eds) *Confronting Consumption*. Cambridge MA and London: The MIT Press, page 46.

NOTES TO CHAPTER 8

1   Korten, David C (2003) "Living Economies for a Living Planet. Part V: Mature Communities and Living Economies". *Simple Living Newsletter*, March-April, page 6. www.simple-living.net

2   Wheatley, Margaret (2006) *Leadership and the New Science: Discovering Order in a Chaotic World*. San Francisco: Berrett-Koehler Publications.

3   Cornelius Castoriadis, cited in Giroux, Henry A (2001) *Public Spaces, Private Lives: Beyond the Culture of Cynicism*. New York: Rowman and Littlefield, page 81.

4   Brandt, Barbara (1995) *Whole Life Economics: Revaluing Daily Life*. Philadelphia, PA and Gabriola Island, BC: New Society Publishers, page 189.

5   Conca, Ken (2002) "Consumption and Environment in a Global Economy", in Princen, Thomas, Maniates, Michael and Conca, Ken (eds) *Confronting Consumption*. Cambridge MA and London: The MIT Press, page 151.

6   The concept of rich choices is developed in Durning, Alan (1992) *How Much is Enough? The Consumer Society and the Fate of the Earth*. New York: Norton, and in
Levett, Roger, with Ian Christie, Michael Jacobs and Riki Therivel (2003) *A Better Choice of Choice: Quality of life, consumption and economic growth*. London: Fabian Society.

7   Conca, Ken (2002) "Consumption and Environment in a

Global Economy", in Princen, Thomas, Maniates, Michael and Conca, Ken (eds) *Confronting Consumption*. Cambridge MA and London: The MIT Press, page 151.

8   McKibben, Bill (2004) *Enough: Genetic Engineering and Human Nature*. London: Bloomsbury, page 203.

9   Durning, Alan (1992) *How Much is Enough? The Consumer Society and the Fate of the Earth*. New York: Norton, pages 25 and 66.

10 Durning, Alan (1992) *How Much is Enough? The Consumer Society and the Fate of the Earth*. New York: Norton, page 25.

11 Andrews, Cecile (2006) *Slow is Beautiful: new visions of community, leisure and joie de vivre*. Gabriola Island, BC: New Society Publishers.

Dawson, Jonathan (2006) *Ecovillages: New Frontiers for Sustainability*. Schumacher Briefings no 7. Totnes, Devon: Green Books.

Hopkins, Rob (2008) *The Transition Handbook: From oil dependency to local resilience*. Totnes: Green Books.

Petrini, Carlo (2001) *Slow Food: Collected Thoughts on Taste, Tradition and the Honest Pleasures of Food*. White River Junction:VT: Chelsea Green Publishing Company.

Also www.slowfood.com

The Simple Living Network www.simpleliving.net

12 Dominguez, Joe and Robin, Vicki (1997, second edition) Your Money or Your Life: *Transforming Your Relationship with Money and Achieving Financial Independence*. Harmondsworth: Penguin.

Naish, John (2008) *Enough: Breaking free from the world of more*. London: Hodder and Stoughton.

Ryan, Anne B (2002) *Balancing Your Life: A Practical Guide to Work, Time, Money and Happiness*. Dublin: The Liffey Press.

Swenson, Richard A. (1998) *The Overload Syndrome: Learning to Live Within Your Limits*. Colorado Springs: Navpress.

13 Tudge, Colin (2007) *Feeding People is Easy*. Pari: Paripublishing,

page 177.

14 Tudge, Colin (2004) *So Shall We Reap: What's gone wrong with the world's food – and how to fix it.* London: Penguin, page 405.

15 Korten, David C (2003) "Living Economies for a Living Planet. Part V: Mature Communities and Living Economies". *Simple Living Newsletter*, March-April, page 2.

16 Meg Wheatley calls this getting the idea into the relational or communication networks, in Wheatley, Margaret (2006) *Leadership and the New Science: Discovering Order in a Chaotic World.* San Francisco: Berrett-Koehler Publications, page 87.

17 Milani, Brian (2002) "From Opposition to Alternatives: Postindustrial Potentials and Transformative Learning", in O'Sullivan, Edmund V., Amish Morell and Mary Ann O'Connor (eds) *Expanding the Boundaries of Transformative Learning.* New York: Palgrave Macmillan, page 50.

18 Goodman, Anne (2003) *Now What? Developing our Future: Understanding our Place in the Unfolding Universe.* New York: Peter Lang, page 19.

19 Selby, David (2002) "The signature of the Whole: Radical Interconnectedness and its Implications for Global and Environmental Education", in O'Sullivan, Edmund V., Amish Morell and Mary Ann O'Connor (eds), *Expanding the Boundaries of Transformative Learning.* New York: Palgrave Macmillan, page 88.

20 Spretnak, Charlene (1999) *The Resurgence of the Real.* New York: Routledge.
McIntosh, Alastair (2001) *Soil and Soul: People versus Corporate Power.* London: Aurum Press

21 Maniates, Michael (2002) "Individualization: Plant a Tree, Buy a Bike, Save the World?" in Princen, Thomas, Maniates, Michael and Conca, Ken (2002) (eds) *Confronting Consumption.* Cambridge MA and London: The MIT Press, page 46.

22 Gottlieb, Roger S. (2003) *A Spirituality of Resistance: Finding a Peaceful Heart and Protecting the Earth.* Lanham, Maryland:

Rowman and Littlefield, page 55.

23 Spretnak, Charlene (1999) *The Resurgence of the Real*. New York: Routledge, page 135.

24 Goodman, Anne (2003) *Now What? Developing our Future: Understanding our Place in the Unfolding Universe*. New York: Peter Lang, page 169.

25 Badaracco, Jospeh (2001) "Beyond Heroic Moral Leadership", *Conversations on Leadership* 2001-2. Harvard: Centre for Public Leadership. www.ksg.harvard.edu/leadership/beyond_heroic_moral _leadership.html. Accessed 24 Sept 2005

26 Sheldrake, Rupert (1995) *Seven Experiments That Could Change the World: A Do-It-Yourself Guide to Revolutionary Science*. New York: Riverhead. Cited in Wheatley, Margaret (2006) *Leadership and the New Science: Discovering Order in a Chaotic World*. San Francisco: Berrett-Koehler Publications, page 53.

27 Gottlieb, Roger S. (2003) *A Spirituality of Resistance: Finding a Peaceful Heart and Protecting the Earth*. Lanham, Maryland: Rowman and Littlefield, page 98.

NOTES TO CHAPTER 9

1 Eagleton, Terry (2003) *After Theory*. Cambridge, MA: Basic Books, page 69.

2 Selby, David (2002) "The signature of the Whole: Radical Interconnectedness and its Implications for Global and Environmental Education", pages 87, 88 in O'Sullivan, Edmund V., Amish Morell and Mary Ann O'Connor (eds), *Expanding the Boundaries of Transformative Learning*. New York: Palgrave Macmillan, pages 77 – 93.

3 Goodman, Anne (2003) *Now What? Developing our Future: Understanding our Place in the Unfolding Universe*. New York: Peter Lang, page 93.

4 Selby, David (2002) "The signature of the Whole: Radical Interconnectedness and its Implications for Global and

Environmental Education", in O'Sullivan, Edmund V., Amish Morell and Mary Ann O'Connor (eds), *Expanding the Boundaries of Transformative Learning*. New York: Palgrave Macmillan, pages 86-87.

5   Palmer, Parker (2000) *Let Your Life Speak: Listening for the Voice of Vocation*. San Francisco: Jossey Bass.

6   Hochschild, Arlie Russell (2003) *The Commercialization of Intimate Life: Notes from Home and Work*. Berkeley: University of California Press, page 87.

7   Eric Fromm, cited in Harding, Stephan (2006) *Animate Earth: Science, Intuition and Gaia*. Totnes: Green Books, page 15.

8   Eagleton, Terry (2003) *After Theory*. Cambridge, MA: Basic Books, page 184.

9   Hochschild, Arlie Russell (2003) *The Commercialization of Intimate Life: Notes from Home and Work*. Berkeley: University of California Press, page 78.

10 Hochschild, Arlie Russell (2003) *The Commercialization of Intimate Life: Notes from Home and Work*. Berkeley: University of California Press, page 77 ff.

11 Gottlieb, Roger S. (2003) *A Spirituality of Resistance: Finding a Peaceful Heart and Protecting the Earth*. Lanham, Maryland: Rowman and Littlefield, page 95.
    Greenspan, Miriam (2004) *Healing Through the Dark Emotions: The Wisdom of Grief, Fear and Despair*. Boston and London: Shambala.
    Lerner, Harriet (2004) *Fear and Other Uninvited Guests*. New York: Harper Collins, page 52.

12 Goodman, Anne (2003) *Now What? Developing our Future: Understanding our Place in the Unfolding Universe*. New York: Peter Lang, page 93.

13 Phillips, Adam (2005) *Going Sane*. London: Hamish Hamilton, page 74.

14 McKibben, Bill (2004) *Enough: Genetic Engineering and Human Nature*. London: Bloomsbury, page 163.

[15] Lamott, Anne (1994) *Some Instructions on Writing and Life*. New York: Doubleday, page 108.

[16] Hochschild, Arlie Russell (2003) *The Commercialization of Intimate Life: Notes from Home and Work*. Berkeley: University of California Press , page 24.

[17] Eagleton, Terry (2003) *After Theory*. Cambridge, MA: Basic Books, page 211.

[18] Hochschild, Arlie Russell (2003) *The Commercialization of Intimate Life: Notes from Home and Work*. Berkeley: University of California Press, pages 213-331.

[19] Lerner, Harriet (2001) *The Dance of Connection*. New York: Harper Collins, page 203.

[20] Eagleton, Terry (2003) *After Theory*. Cambridge, MA: Basic Books, page 168ff.

[21] Hochschild, Arlie Russell (2003) *The Commercialization of Intimate Life: Notes from Home and Work*. Berkeley: University of California Press, page 123.

[22] Phillips, Adam (2005) *Going Sane*. London: Hamish Hamilton, page 229.

[23] Palmer, Parker (2000) *Let Your Life Speak: Listening for the Voice of Vocation*. San Francisco: Jossey Bass, page 93.

[24] Lamott, Anne (1994) *Some Instructions on Writing and Life*. New York: Doubleday, pages 205-6.

[25] Palmer, Parker (2000) *Let Your Life Speak: Listening for the Voice of Vocation*. San Francisco: Jossey Bass, pages 92-93.
Palmer, Parker (2004) *A Hidden Wholeness: The Journey Towards an Undivided Life*. San Francisco: Jossey Bass, page 182.

[26] Palmer, Parker (2000) *Let Your Life Speak: Listening for the Voice of Vocation*. San Francisco: Jossey Bass, page 92.

[27] Eagleton, Terry (2003) *After Theory*. Cambridge, MA: Basic Books, page 212.

[28] Phillips, Adam (2005) *Going Sane*. London: Hamish Hamilton, page 245.

NOTES TO CONCLUSION

1 Phillips, Adam (2005) *Going Sane*. London: Hamish Hamilton, page 103.

BOOKS

O is a symbol of the world, of oneness and unity. In different cultures it also means the "eye," symbolizing knowledge and insight. We aim to publish books that are accessible, constructive and that challenge accepted opinion, both that of academia and the "moral majority."

Our books are available in all good English language bookstores worldwide. If you don't see the book on the shelves ask the bookstore to order it for you, quoting the ISBN number and title. Alternatively you can order online (all major online retail sites carry our titles) or contact the distributor in the relevant country, listed on the copyright page.

See our website www.o-books.net for a full list of over 500 titles, growing by 100 a year.

And tune in to myspiritradio.com for our book review radio show, hosted by June-Elleni Laine, where you can listen to the authors discussing their books.

MySpiritRadio